Medical Care Provided Under California's Workers' Compensation Program

Effects of the Reforms and Additional Opportunities to Improve the Quality and Efficiency of Care

Barbara O. Wynn, Justin William Timbie, Melony E. Sorbero

Prepared for the Commission on Health and Safety and Workers' Compensation

CENTER FOR HEALTH AND SAFETY IN THE WORKPLACE

A study by the RAND Institute for Civil Justice and RAND Health

This research was prepared for the Commission on Health and Safety and Workers' Compensation and was conducted under the auspices of the Center for Health and Safety in the Workplace.

Library of Congress Cataloging-in-Publication Data is available for this publication

ISBN: 978-0-8330-5836-2

The RAND Corporation is a nonprofit institution that helps improve policy and decisionmaking through research and analysis. RAND's publications do not necessarily reflect the opinions of its research clients and sponsors.

RAND® is a registered trademark.

Published 2011 by the RAND Corporation
1776 Main Street, P.O. Box 2138, Santa Monica, CA 90407-2138
1200 South Hayes Street, Arlington, VA 22202-5050
4570 Fifth Avenue, Suite 600, Pittsburgh, PA 15213-2665
RAND URL: http://www.rand.org/
To order RAND documents or to obtain additional information, contact
Distribution Services: Telephone: (310) 451-7002;
Fax: (310) 451-6915; Email: order@rand.org

Preface

Since 2004, significant changes have been made to the California workers' compensation (WC) system. The Commission on Health and Safety and Workers' Compensation (CHSWC) asked the RAND Corporation to examine the impact that these changes have on the medical care provided to injured workers. This monograph synthesizes findings from interviews with knowledgeable individuals and available information regarding the implementation of the changes affecting WC medical care and identifies areas in which additional changes might increase the quality and efficiency of care delivered under the WC system. The monograph should be of broad interest to stakeholders in California's WC system and in other WC programs in other states.

This research was undertaken for CHSWC over a five-year period. It was conducted under the umbrella of the RAND Center for Health and Safety in the Workplace.

The RAND Center for Health and Safety in the Workplace

The RAND Center for Health and Safety in the Workplace is dedicated to reducing workplace injuries and illnesses. The center provides objective, innovative, cross-cutting research to improve understanding of the complex network of issues that affect occupational safety, health, and WC. Its vision is to become the nation's leader in improving workers' health and safety policy.

The center draws on expertise within three RAND research units:

- RAND Institute for Civil Justice, a national leader in research on WC
- RAND Health, the most trusted source of objective health policy research in the world
- RAND Infrastructure, Safety, and Environment, a national leader in research on occupational safety.

The center's work is supported by funds from federal, state, and private sources.

For additional information about the center, please contact the director:

John Mendeloff, Director
Center for Health and Safety in the Workplace
RAND Corporation
4570 Fifth Avenue, Suite 600
Pittsburgh, PA 15213-2665
(412) 683-2300, x4532

- (412) 683-2800 fax
- John_Mendeloff@rand.org

For additional information about this monograph, please contact the principal investigator:

Barbara O. Wynn, Senior Policy Analyst
RAND Corporation
1200 South Hayes Street
Arlington, VA 22202-5050
(703) 413-1100, x5413
Barbara_Wynn@rand.org

Contents

Figures

Tables

Summary

California's WC system was at the center of intense debate and legislative activity during the period leading up to reforms in 2003 and 2004. High rates of growth in medical care expenditures stimulated a series of reform efforts to control medical-treatment expenses for injured workers and to improve program efficiency. CHSWC asked RAND to examine the impact that such policy changes could have on the medical care provided to injured workers. This monograph focuses on policies and incentives in the postreform period that affected the use and costs of care and recommends policy changes that would improve the quality and efficiency of care.

Key Reform Provisions

The most-important new policies affecting the medical treatment provided to injured workers were the following:

- Adopt medical-treatment guidelines as presumptively correct medical treatment. Previously, the medical decisions of the primary treating physician were presumptively correct.
- Limit chiropractic, physical therapy, and occupational therapy services to 24 visits per industrial injury.
- Require that injured workers of employers with medical provider networks (MPNs) use network providers throughout the course of their treatment. If the employer does not have an MPN, the prior rules remain in effect that allow the employer to control provider choice for the first 30 days and permit the injured worker to choose the primary treating physician after 30 days.
- Establish new standards for utilization review (UR) processes.
- Create a second-opinion program for spinal surgery.
- Revise the Official Medical Fee Schedule (OMFS) to do the following:
  - Include additional inpatient hospital services facility and facility fees for outpatient surgery and emergency services, and provide for annual updates for inflation and other changes based on 120 percent of Medicare fee-schedule amounts.
  - Lower allowable fees for pharmaceuticals to Medi-Cal rates, and require generic drugs.
  - Reduce physician fees 5 percent, and authorize the administrative director (AD) of the Division of Workers' Compensation (DWC) to implement a new fee schedule for physician services.

Purpose and Approach

Our purpose in this study was to analyze the effects that these new policies had on access to medically appropriate care and efficiency of service delivery. We also recommend additional changes that might increase both quality and efficiency of care in California's WC system. We were unable to obtain access to longitudinal claim-level data spanning the prepost reform periods that are needed to analyze fully the legislative changes' impacts on medical treatment provided to injured workers. As a result, we focused on how the reforms affect access to medically appropriate care and its quality and efficiency. Specifically, we addressed the following questions:

- What has been the reform provisions' impact on overall medical expenditures and on the use and payments for major types of services? Would additional policy changes improve the quality or efficiency of care, reduce administrative burden, or improve program oversight?
- What has been the experience to date with medical provider networks? Should additional policy changes be considered to improve the performance of medical provider networks?
- What has been the reform provisions' impact on medical cost-containment expenses and selected activities, i.e., UR and resolving medical-necessity disputes? Would additional policy changes increase administrative efficiency?
- Is it feasible to use the WC information system (WCIS) to establish an ongoing system for monitoring access to medically appropriate care? What are its limitations, and how might they be addressed?

To address these questions, we pursued several approaches. We conducted interviews with knowledgeable individuals involved in the WC medical-treatment system from different perspectives: self-insured employers, payers, providers, applicants' attorneys, state regulators, WC appeals judges, and researchers. We also conducted a literature review of pertinent reports and regulations involving WC in California and other states. And we analyzed two kinds of administrative data: data from California's Office of Statewide Health Planning and Development on inpatient hospital services, ambulatory surgery facility services, and emergency room services provided to WC patients; and medical-service data for services provided in 2007 by WCIS, the first full calendar year for which data have been submitted.

We summarize here what we learned about the reforms' effect on the utilization and costs of care, medical provider networks, and administrative processes and expenses.

Utilization and Costs of Care

Our examination of overall changes in annual medical expenditures for WC medical care shows the following:

- Total annual paid medical losses fell sharply following implementation of the reform provisions but have been rising since 2008. These aggregate losses have been affected not only by the medical-reform provisions but also by significant reductions in the number of WC claims.

- Reduced payments to providers were the major contributing factor to the initial reductions in annual paid losses. Subsequently, expenses for actual medical care have been rising less rapidly than expenses related to administration of the medical benefit, such as medical cost-containment expenses, medical-legal expenses, and direct payments to workers (which are mostly claim settlements).
- Paid medical losses remain significantly lower than they would have been in the absence of the reform provisions but continue to be higher than those of WC programs in other states.

Since it unlikely that the reduction in the number of new WC claims is related to implementation of the reform provisions, per-claim measures of medical expenses might be more relevant than the measures of aggregate expenditures. In this regard, one important metric is average paid medical losses by accident year at a common maturity date. For insured claims involving indemnity payments for temporary or permanent disability, the average first 12 months of paid medical losses were at their lowest level in accident year 2005 and subsequently have been increasing 13.1 percent annually. Further research is needed to determine how the decline in WC claims has affected cost trends and the severity of injuries.

Physician and Other Practitioner Services

Physician and other practitioner services were most affected by the changes in medical-treatment policies, especially policies that required the adoption of medical-treatment guidelines and the limitation on chiropractic, physical therapy, and occupational therapy services to 24 visits per industrial injury. Estimated system-wide payments (by insurers and self-insured employers) for physician and practitioner services declined from a high of $3.7 billion in 2003 to $2.1 billion in 2009.

Stakeholders interviewed in 2006–2007 believed that the guidelines were well designed for acute conditions but were deficient for not addressing chronic pain, alternative therapies, and use of pharmaceuticals. These concerns have largely been addressed through additional guidelines for acupuncture and chronic pain, although it is too early to assess the impact of these new guidelines.

However, two other concerns expressed by stakeholders might remain applicable. First, concerns were often expressed not about the guidelines per se but that they were being applied too stringently during UR and that insufficient attention was paid to the individual patient's condition that might warrant deviation from the guidelines. Second, there were some concerns that the Labor Code requirement that any medical guidelines to be adopted must be evidence based, nationally recognized, and peer reviewed precluded providing needed guidelines for therapies that do not have a robust evidence base. This issue has most recently arisen with respect to compound drugs and medical foods, for which there is limited evidence on which to establish guidelines.

In 2007, overall utilization of physician and other practitioner services in California during the first 12 months of a claim fell from being about 50 percent more than the median for a multistate comparison group in the prereform period to slightly less than the median. Impact of the changes was greatest on chiropractic care, an estimated 81-percent reduction in total payments between 2003 and 2009 that reflects the imposition of the 24-visit-per-injury limitation and the impact of the American College of Occupational and Environmental Medicine (ACOEM) guidelines. California continues to use substantially more evaluation and management (E/M) services than other states with about the same number of visits per claim as preform.

The current fee schedule is outdated and should be replaced by a resource-based fee schedule that creates better incentives to provide appropriate care, by aligning payments with the costs of care. In the aggregate, the allowances for practitioner services are currently about 111 percent of the Medicare fee-schedule rates, which is a lower differential than is allowed for the fee schedules for hospital and ambulatory surgery facility services. Because having high-quality physicians is fundamental to increasing the value of medical care provided under the WC system, paying relatively less for physician services than other services is short sighted. In lieu of across-the-board increases for E/M services, it might be more effective to create payments for activities that are unique to work-related injuries. For example, Washington's quality-improvement initiative reimbursed physicians for calls to employers of injured workers to coordinate return to work and rewarded physicians who filed timely reports (Wickizer, Franklin, et al., 2004).

Inpatient Hospital and Ambulatory Surgery Services

Expenditures for inpatient hospital services declined with the expansion of the OMFS to high-cost inpatient services, such as trauma and burns, but they have since risen above preform levels because of regular updates for inflation and other factors. We identified two potential inefficiencies: a duplicate payment for hardware implanted during spinal surgery and the inflationary impact of improvements in coding that increase payments without a corresponding increase in the costs of care.

The OMFS was also expanded to cover facility fees for ambulatory surgery services provided by hospitals and freestanding ambulatory surgery centers, which have a lower cost structure than hospitals. Paying a lower rate to freestanding surgery centers would increase the value of those services and reduce the incentive to shift care inappropriately from hospitals and physician offices. The savings from eliminating unnecessary institutional expenditures could be used to reduce employer costs or increase payments to physicians and other practitioners.

Outpatient Drugs and Other Pharmaceuticals

Despite the reform provisions affecting outpatient drugs, there has been significant growth in both the average number of prescriptions and the average payment per claim for prescriptions (Swedlow, Ireland, and Gardner, 2009). One cause for the increase is physician-dispensed compound drugs, and convenience packaging of drugs and medical foods (co-packs). Another important contributing factor has been a growing use of Schedule II medications (drugs with accepted medical use that have a high potential for abuse or addiction). Both issues were addressed to some extent in the medical-treatment guidelines that were issued in 2007 for chronic pain. It is too early to know how effectively the guidelines will address the pharmaceutical overuse issues, but it appears that that additional guidelines are needed to address compound drugs and medical foods and that OMFS changes are needed to ensure that allowances for these products are reasonable. However, the experience with earlier attempts to address pharmaceutical overuse suggests that the benefits gained from making these policy changes are likely to be temporary unless greater attention is given to improving the overall physician incentives.

Medical Provider Networks

Under the reform provisions, a self-insured employer or insurer may establish an MPN to provide care to injured workers throughout their course of medical treatment. Unless a worker has predesignated a personal physician as his or her primary-care physician prior to his or her injury, the employer assigns the worker to a network physician for initial medical treatment. The worker is free to choose another provider within the network after the first visit but has very limited rights to receive out-of-network care.

As of March 2011, there are 1,401 active MPNs. The MPN penetration rate is uncertain, but it appears that most care is provided under either an MPN contract or another type of contract. The combined proportion of payments made under MPNs and other contracts for accident year (AY) 2007 is 59 percent and lower for older claims. Currently, most MPNs are broad panels selected primarily to meet access requirements and provide fee-discounting opportunities. A few payers—most notably, some self-insured employers—have contracted selectively with providers.

With a few notable exceptions, another administrative entity usually forms the MPN and contracted directly with network physicians. The payer contracts with that administrative entity to "lease" the provider network and does not directly contract with the physicians. The administrative entity leases the same network to multiple payers, resulting in different payers applying for MPN approval for the same group of providers. This creates unnecessary administrative burden and makes it difficult to assess the performance of individual MPNs. As a practical matter, accountability for network performance is not clearly established, and information needed to assess adequacy of network coverage is not obtained. Reapproval is required when there is a material modification (including a 10-percent change in network providers), but there is no recertification process, and the AD has no intermediate sanctions for poor performance—termination is the only recourse for MPNs that fail to meet the required standards.

These shortcomings could be remedied through changes in the Labor Code. The most important change would be to change the definition of the applicant for MPN approval to be the group of providers or entity that establishes the MPN (employer, insurer, or other administrative entity). This would streamline the approval process and better align legal accountability with operational accountability for meeting MPN standards.

Other issues that were identified during our interviews and potential changes to address them include the following:

- The employer or insurer has the exclusive right to determine the members of its network but is not explicitly relieved of the burden of proving that due process was used in the provider selection process. The Labor Code provision that allows the payer to be selective in provider contracting could be strengthened.
- When provider networks are leased, a provider might not be aware of its responsibilities as an MPN provider. A written agreement could be required between the MPN and network physician outlining the physician's responsibilities as a network provider.
- Most workers either are not aware of the right to predesignate or do not anticipate that they will have an injury that they would like to have treated by their personal physician. The Labor Code could be revised to allow an injured worker to designate his or her per-

sonal physician as primary treating physician after an injury occurs if the physician agrees to abide by the MPN rules and refer only to the MPN.

Medical Cost-Containment Expenses and Activities

Medical cost-containment activities are payer actions to monitor and manage the price, use, and volume of medical services and products based on clinical efficiency and need. The expenses for these activities have risen rapidly since the implementation of the reform provisions. Because the categories of expenses are not reported separately, it is difficult to determine the reasons for the increases, although it appears that major factors are expenses incurred for leasing MPNs and costs associated with medical-necessity determinations.

In our stakeholder interviews, providers raised considerable concern over the UR process. Major concerns included the application of the medical-treatment guidelines as "hard and fast" rules with reluctance to approve any deviations from the guidelines, across-the-board review of all services, and excessive and unreasonable levels of documentation being required to substantiate medical necessity. Results from a University of Washington provider survey found that at least four of the top five barriers to care cited by physicians were related to the UR process and strict application of the medical-treatment guidelines.

It is difficult to analyze decisions made during the UR process because most care is reviewed prospectively and might never enter the bill processing or appeal processes. DWC undertakes routine UR investigations that but do inform whether UR procedural requirements are being followed and provide an overview of the types of UR reviews and decisions but do not address the quality of the decisionmaking process. Summary measures are reported for the timeliness of the responses, whether the content of the notice was proper, and whether the notice was distributed to the proper individuals. Most faulty responses involved timeliness of decisions (7.5 percent of cases). Overall, 7.5 percent of decisions involved an untimely response.

In our interviews, some stakeholders expressed concerns about the complexity, timeliness, and appropriateness of the dispute-resolution process for medical-necessity determinations. The current independent medical review process for MPN medical-necessity disputes is not functional because workers may simply keep changing physicians when there is a dispute over appropriate medical care. A large share of expedited hearings and many regular hearings involve medical-necessity issues. When these issues reach hearings, judges make decisions based on their understanding of evidence presented to them, but the rulings on these issues are not decided by medical experts in the medical treatment at issue.

Potentially, external review of medical-necessity issues could reduce the complexity of California's dispute-resolution process, increase the timeliness and appropriateness of medical-necessity appeal determinations, and reduce medical cost-containment expenses. There are various models that use external review organizations in deciding medical-necessity disputes. Timely and impartial independent medical review (IMR) decisions would improve the quality of medical-necessity decisions because such issues would be decided by medical experts instead of judges in an administrative process. To reinforce the use of the IMR process, a limit could be established on the number of times the worker may change physicians within the same specialty without MPN permission (e.g., several states provide that the employee may change initial provider twice and authorized specialist twice). This would encourage resolution of medical-necessity issues through the dispute-resolution process rather than through switching providers and reduce inefficiencies inherent in changing physicians.

Monitoring System Performance Through the Workers' Compensation Information System

The overarching purpose of performance-measurement systems is to provide information that will enable policymakers and other stakeholders to identify areas in which performance is suboptimal. This then allows for the prioritization of identified issues, as well as the development of policies and interventions that will facilitate improvements in performance. These same systems can then be used to evaluate the effects of reforms and interventions.

Complete and reliable reporting to the WCIS is key to DWC's ability to monitor performance. Medical data reporting is required for all services provided on or after September 22, 2006. DWC reports that WCIS data are incomplete, with approximately 11–12 percent of claims not reported into the sytem and further underreporting of medical data (California Department of Industrial Relations, 2011). Section 138.6 of the Labor Code, which sets out the AD's authority with respect to reporting requirements for the WCIS, does not include penalties for the failure of a claim administrator to comply with the electronic data-reporting requirements. Notably, two of the three other states with medical data-reporting requirements (Florida and Texas) both have financial penalties associated with failure to comply with reporting compliance. Texas has very high compliance rates; achieving such rates is likely possible only when requirements are paired with financial penalties for noncompliance. (Like California, Oregon does not have any penalties.)

There are many significant challenges to implementing a performance-monitoring system that focuses on the quality of medical care delivered to injured workers. To date, very few measures assessing the appropriateness of care can be supported using only medical data. These, combined with measures of utilization selected with input from providers and other stakeholders for common types of WC illnesses and injuries, could form the initial efforts to measure performance. These efforts could be enhanced and built upon as new measures become available and the use of electronic medical records becomes common. As more information is reported through other measurement activities, such as the Centers for Medicare and Medicaid Services (CMS) Physician Quality Reporting System, the feasibility and stakeholder receptiveness to the inclusion of data reported to national performance-assessment efforts supported by all-payer data (as opposed to data on WC payers alone) in a WC monitoring system should be assessed.

Recommendations

The medical-treatment system for WC is complex and multifaceted. We have limited our review to selected aspects of the system that were affected by the reform provisions and areas in which we believe further policy changes would improve system performance. The following recommendations would improve the incentives for providing medically appropriate care efficiently, increase accountability for performance, facilitate DWC monitoring and oversight, and reduce administrative burden.

Create Incentives for Providing Medically Appropriate Care Efficiently

The value of medical treatment would be improved by doing the following:

- Implement a resource-based fee schedule that provides for regular updates and equitable payment levels.
- Create nonmonetary incentives for providing medically appropriate care. Within the MPN context, incentives could be created through more-selective contracting with providers and reducing UR and prior-authorization requirements for high-performing physicians.
- Reduce unnecessary expenditures for inpatient hospital care by eliminating the duplicate payment for spinal hardware and the inflationary impact of coding improvement.
- Reduce unnecessary expenditures for ambulatory surgery by reducing the OMFS multiplier for procedures performed in freestanding ambulatory surgery centers.
- Reduce the incentives for inappropriate prescribing practices by curtailing in-office physician dispensing.
- Implement the pharmacy benefit network provisions.

Increase Accountability for Performance

Accountability for performance could be increased by making the following revisions in the Labor Code:

- Revise the MPN certification process to place accountability for meeting MPN standards on the entity contracting with the physician network.
- Strengthen DWC authorities to do the following:
  - Provide intermediate sanctions for failure to comply with MPN requirements.
  - Provide penalties for the failure of a claim administrator to comply with the data-reporting requirements.
- Modify the Labor Code to remove payers and MPNs from the definition of *individually identifiable data* so that performance on key measures can be publicly available.

Facilitate Monitoring and Oversight

Program oversight activities could be facilitated by the following:

- Provide DWC with more flexibility to add needed data elements to medical data reporting, e.g., revise the WCIS reporting requirements to require a unique identifier for each MPN.
- Require that medical cost-containment expenses be reported by category of cost (e.g., bill review, network leasing, UR, case management).
- Compile information on the types of medical services that are subject to UR denials and expedited hearings.
- Expand ongoing monitoring of system performance.

Increase Administrative Efficiency

Efficiency in the administration of medical benefits could be increased by the following:

- Use an external medical review organization to review medical-necessity determinations. A separate dispute-resolution process for medical-necessity determinations also creates a mechanism to monitor the quality of payer decisions and to identify areas in which expansions or revisions in the MTUS are needed.
- Explore best practices of other WC programs and health programs in carrying out medical cost-containment activities.

Issues Needing Additional Research

There are several aspects of the medical-treatment system that warrant additional investigation.

Cost of Care. An increased understanding of the reasons behind the postreform changes in the costs of medical care is needed. This could be done by decomposing the WC cost experience into various components: price, utilization, claim volume and mix (industry and type of injury), and benchmarking the results to relevant WC and other health program experience. In the short run, this type of comparison will help explain the factors contributing to the changes in annual paid losses. In the long run, the methods developed to do so could be incorporated into a performance-monitoring system.

Quality of Care. With regard to quality of care, there are many significant challenges to developing appropriate measures for a performance-monitoring system. To date, very few measures assessing the appropriateness of care can be supported using only medical data. These, combined with utilization measures selected with input from providers and other stakeholders for common types of WC illnesses and injuries, could form the initial efforts to measure performance. These efforts could be enhanced and built upon as new measures become available and the use of electronic medical records becomes common. As more information is reported through other measurement activities, such as the CMS Physician Quality Reporting System, the feasibility and stakeholder receptiveness to the inclusion of data reported to national performance-assessment efforts supported by all-payer data in a WC monitoring system should be assessed.

Work-Related Outcomes of Care. The literature concerning the impact of the reform provisions has focused on changes in the use and costs of medical services. Additional work is needed to understand how work-related outcomes, such as days lost from work and return to work, are affected by differences in patterns of service. This type of analysis will require linking transaction-level medical data with other administrative data sets.

Comparative Performance. On the basis of our stakeholder interviews, we identified selective contracting as an MPN best practice. Further research is needed to compare the pattern and costs of care under different contracting arrangements and to assess whether the narrow WC networks have better outcomes and cost-efficiency than broad networks.

Acknowledgments

We are extremely grateful for the valuable support and thoughtful guidance that we received throughout this study from our project officer, Christine Baker, executive officer of CHSWC. We also appreciate the support that Lachlan Taylor and Irina Nemirovsky of the CHSWC staff provided throughout the study and the efforts of the DWC research staff that made our analysis of their medical data possible: Martha Jones, David Henderson, Lisa Dasinger, and Genet Daba. We would also like to thank the many stakeholders and knowledgeable observers of the California WC system who willingly shared their insights and experiences throughout the project.

We appreciate the information-gathering and data-analysis assistance provided in the early stages of the project by Rebecca Nolind Shaw and Beth Ann Griffin, both at RAND, and Sarah Zakowski (then at RAND) and, in the later stages, by Christina Walker (then at RAND) and Susan Lovejoy, also at RAND. We thank RAND colleague Lawrence Painter for applying his programming expertise to the analysis of the WCIS data. We also appreciate the thoughtful comments and insights provided by Frank Neuhauser, executive director of the Center for the Study of Social Insurance at the University of California, Berkeley, and our RAND colleagues Carole Roan Gresenz and Laura Zakaras on an earlier version of this monograph. Finally, we thank Melissa Ko for her help in preparation of the document and Michelle Platt for her ongoing administrative support throughout the project.

Abbreviations

AAAASF	American Association for Accreditation of Ambulatory Surgery Facilities
AAAHC	Accreditation Association for Ambulatory Health Care
AB	assembly bill
ACOEM	American College of Occupational and Environmental Medicine
AD	administrative director
ALIRTS	Automated Licensing Information and Report Tracking System
AME	agreed medical evaluator
APC	ambulatory payment classification
ASC	ambulatory surgical center
AY	accident year
BETOS	Berenson-Eggers Type of Service
CAH	critical-access hospital
CC	complication or comorbidity
CHCF	California HealthCare Foundation
CHSWC	Commission on Health and Safety and Workers' Compensation
CMI	case-mix index
CMS	Centers for Medicare and Medicaid Services
CPI	Consumer Price Index
CPT	Current Procedural Terminology
CT	computerized tomography
CWCI	California Workers' Compensation Institute
DN	data number
DO	

DRG	diagnosis-related group
DWC	Division of Workers' Compensation
ECMO	extracorporeal membrane oxygenation
ED	emergency department
EDI	electronic data interchange
FDA	U.S. Food and Drug Administration
FROI	first report of injury
FY	fiscal year
HCO	health care organization
HCPCS	Healthcare Common Procedure Coding System
HOPD	hospital outpatient department
IAIABC	International Association of Industrial Accident Boards and Commissions
ICD-9-CM	International Classification of Diseases, 9th Revision, Clinical Modification
ICSI	Institute for Clinical Systems Improvement
IMR	independent medical reviewer
IMRO	independent medical review organization
IOM	Institute of Medicine
IRF	inpatient rehabilitation facility
JCN	jurisdiction claim number
MCC	major complication or comorbidity
MCO	managed care organization
MDC	major diagnostic category
MedPAC	Medicare Payment Advisory Commission
MIRCal	Medical Information Reporting for California
MLR	medical loss ratio
MPN	medical provider network
MRI	magnetic resonance imaging
MS-DRG	Medicare severity-adjusted diagnosis-related group
MTUS	medical treatment utilization schedule
MV	mechanical ventilation

NASI   National Academy of Social Insurance

NCQA   National Committee for Quality Assurance

NYU   New York University

OMFS   Official Medical Fee Schedule

OPPS   Outpatient Prospective Payment System

OR   operating room

OSHPD   Office of Statewide Health Planning and Development

PDX   principal diagnosis

PPO   preferred-provider organization

PPS   prospective payment system

PQRI   Physician Quality Reporting Initiative

QME   qualified medical examiner

SB   senate bill

TDI   Texas Department of Insurance

UR   utilization review

URAC   Utilization Review Accreditation Commission

WC   workers' compensation

WCAB   Workers' Compensation Appeals Board

WCIRB   Workers' Compensation Insurance Rating Bureau of California

WCIS   workers' compensation information system

WCRI   Workers Compensation Research Institute

CHAPTER ONE

Introduction

Since 2004, significant changes have been made to the California workers' compensation (WC) system. Before the reforms, payments for medical care had been increasing twice as quickly as indemnity payments for temporary and permanent disability. The policies adopted in 2003–2004 were intended to control both indemnity payments and medical-treatment expenses for injured workers and improve program efficiency. Average medical losses per indemnity claim at 12 months valuation were at their lowest level immediately after the implementation of the reform provisions in 2005. Since then, the expenses per indemnity claim have increased 13.1 percent annually. This higher rate of growth prompts concerns about whether further policy changes are needed to create better incentives for the efficient delivery of high-quality care under California's WC program.

The Commission on Health and Safety and Workers' Compensation (CHSWC) asked RAND to examine the impact that the policy changes could have on the medical care provided to injured workers and recommend additional changes to improve the system's performance. This monograph synthesizes research carried out over several years, some of which was previously reported in working papers. We were not able to obtain access to the kind of longitudinal data needed to compare the medical treatment injured workers received before and after the reforms and have used a variety of approaches to analyze the new policies' effects on access to medically appropriate care and efficiency of service delivery. We also recommend additional changes might increase the quality and efficiency of medical care delivered under the WC system.

Background

California's WC program provides medical care and wage-replacement benefits to workers who suffer on-the-job injuries and illnesses. Injured workers are entitled to receive all medical care reasonably required to cure or relieve the effects of their injury with no deductibles or copayments. It is a "no-fault" system that is intended to ensure that workers receive prompt medical attention and needed income protection while shielding employers from liability for civil damages and costly litigation over responsibility for workplace accidents. About 15.2 million workers in California are covered by WC insurance. More than 533,600 claims were filed in 2009 for WC benefits related to workplace injuries and illnesses. Approximately 70 percent of the claims are for employees covered through insurance policies issued by about 100 private for-profit insurers and one public nonprofit insurer, which accounted for about 16 percent of written premium in the insured market in 2010 (California Department of Insurance, undated).

The remaining 30 percent are covered through self-insurance, including 4 percent by the State of California (CHSWC, 2010b).

California's system for delivering WC medical care involves a primary treating physician, who has responsibility for the injured worker's medical care. In addition to providing medical services, the primary treating physician has a central role in determining whether the worker's illness or injury is work related, establishing the plan of treatment and making referrals for specialized care, and assessing readiness to return to work. Care should be consistent with the medical treatment utilization schedule (MTUS) adopted by the administrative director (AD) of the Division of Workers' Compensation (DWC). DWC also maintains an Official Medical Fee Schedule (OMFS) to set the maximum allowable amounts that may be paid to providers for medical services. The OMFS does not apply if the payer (insurer or self-insured employer) has contracted with a provider for a different payment amount.

California's WC program was the center of intense debate and legislative activity during the period leading up to reforms in 2003 and 2004. Rising costs stimulated a series of reform efforts to control both indemnity payments and medical-treatment expenses for injured workers and to improve program efficiency. The most-important reform provisions affecting the medical treatment provided injured workers were to do the following:

- Adopt medical-treatment guidelines as presumptively correct medical treatment. Previously, the medical decisions of the primary treating physician were presumptively correct.
- Limit chiropractic, physical therapy, and occupational therapy services to 24 visits each per industrial injury.
- Require that injured workers of employers with medical provider networks (MPNs) use network providers throughout the course of their treatment. If the employer does not have an MPN, the prior rules remain in effect that allow the employer to control provider choice for the first 30 days and permit the injured worker to choose the primary treating physician after 30 days.
- Establish new standards for utilization review (UR) processes.
- Create a second-opinion program for spinal surgery.
- Revise and expand the OMFS to provide for Medicare-based fee schedules for services other than physician services and pharmaceutical services. With respect to these services, do the following:
  - Reduce physician fees up to 5 percent, and authorize DWC to implement a new fee schedule for physician services.
  - Lower allowable fees for pharmaceuticals to Medi-Cal rates, and require generic drugs.
- Require employers to pay up to $10,000 for medical care before a determination is made regarding the claim's compensability under WC.

Many of these provisions are discussed in greater detail in the remainder of this monograph. Although the monograph's focus is on selected provisions affecting medical care, there are interactions between these provisions and provisions affecting indemnity payments that have an impact on medical expenditures and work-related outcomes. Most notably, the recent legislation also established a two-year limit on temporary disability payments, made significant changes in how permanent disability is defined and apportioned between work-related and non–work-related causes, and created incentives for employers to facilitate return to work.

Purpose

The purpose of this study was to examine selected issues related to the reform provisions' effect on medical care and to identify areas in which additional changes might add value by improving the quality or efficiency (or both) of care provided to injured workers. The study questions include the following:

- What has been the impact on the utilization of the major types of medical services and the payments for those services? In particular, what has been the impact on the use and payments for physician and other practitioner services, inpatient hospital services, ambulatory surgery facility services, and outpatient drugs? Would additional policy changes improve the quality or efficiency of care, reduce administrative burden, or improve program oversight?
- What has been the experience to date with MPNs? Have MPNs affected injured worker access to medically appropriate care? Would additional policy changes improve the quality or efficiency of care provided through MPNs, reduce administrative burden, or improve program oversight?
- What has been the reform provisions' impact on medical cost-containment activities and expenses? What has been the experience to date with the new processes for UR and resolving medical-necessity disputes? Would additional policy changes reduce administrative burden or improve program oversight of medical cost-containment activities?
- Is it feasible to use the WC information system (WCIS) to establish an ongoing system for monitoring access to medically appropriate care? What are its limitations, and how might they be addressed?

Data and Methods

We undertook several types of activities in conducting this analysis. First, we interviewed knowledgeable individuals involved in the WC medical-treatment system from different perspectives: self-insured employers, payers, providers, applicants' attorneys, state regulators, WC appeals judges, and researchers. At the outset of the study (from September 2006 through July 2007), we used a semistructured protocol that asked interviewees about their perceptions of reform provisions' effects on medical care provided to California's injured workers, their overall assessment of whether workers have adequate access to appropriate care, and the strengths and weaknesses of the current system. As issues were identified and investigated during the remainder of the study, we conducted additional interviews that focused on policies and processes used in other states that might be considered as potential "best practices" to improve the administration of California's WC medical benefits.

Second, we conducted an initial and ongoing literature review through Internet searches and periodic checking of the websites of several organizations involved in WC in California and in other states, to gather any pertinent reports, analyses, and regulations. These organizations included the following:

- CHSWC, a joint labor-management body charged with overseeing the health, safety, and WC systems in California

- DWC, the regulatory agency responsible for monitoring the administration of WC claims and providing administrative and judicial services to assist in resolving disputes
- agencies responsible for administering WC medical benefits in other states
- the Workers' Compensation Insurance Rating Bureau of California (WCIRB), a licensed rating organization that collects premium and loss data on all California WC insurance policies and recommends advisory pure premium rates to the California Department of Insurance
- the California Workers' Compensation Institute (CWCI), a nonprofit organization of insurers and self-insured employers that conducts research and analysis to improve the operation of the California WC system
- the Workers Compensation Research Institute (WCRI), a nonprofit independent research organization that produces multistate tracking reports and analyses of WC systems
- the National Academy of Social Insurance (NASI), a nonprofit organization of experts on social insurance that provides annual reports on state-level estimates of WC payments.

These organizations also produce reports that offer empirical data and research performed under their auspices. For example, CWCI maintains a proprietary, transaction-level database on more than 3 million California WC claims contributed by its members for claims with dates of injury between January 1993 and June 2010. CWCI has issued a series of reports tracking trends in medical expenditures and utilization that we reviewed in preparing this monograph. Other important sources of information have been two DWC-sponsored surveys of injured workers, providers, and employers. The first survey was conducted by the Center for Health Policy at the University of California at Los Angeles to assess injured workers' access to appropriate medical care (Kominski et al., 2007); the second survey was conducted by the University of Washington School of Public Health (Wickizer, Sears, et al., 2009).

Our third activity was to analyze available administrative data pertaining to medical care provided under the WC program. We used data from California's Office of Statewide Health Planning and Development (OSHPD) on inpatient hospital services, ambulatory surgery facility services and emergency room services provided to WC patients. The WCIS has data on medical services provided on or after September 22, 2006. For this monograph, we analyzed medical-expenditure data for services provided in 2007, the first full calendar year for which data have been submitted.

Organization of This Monograph

The remaining chapters in this monograph are organized as follows:

- Chapter Two provides an overview of the implementation timeline for the medical reform provisions and examines medical-expenditure trends.
- Chapter Three extends the analysis of medical expenses, first providing background information on the composition of expenses for medical care. The chapter then focuses on changes in the use and cost of the four major types of medical services: services furnished by physicians and other practitioners, inpatient hospital services, ambulatory surgery facility fees, and outpatient drugs and other pharmaceuticals. For each category, the chapter discusses the most-relevant reform provisions affecting the provision of services,

examines available data on the trends in service use and payments, and identifies policy changes that could improve the quality or efficiency of care.

- Chapter Four examines the experience to date with MPNs. After providing overviews of the relevant reform provisions and the MPN landscape, the chapter explores the networks' impact on access and the quality and cost of care. It concludes with a discussion of best practices and policy changes that would improve network operations and program oversight.
- Chapter Five examines the changes that have occurred in medical cost-containment expenses. It then examines in greater detail several medical cost-containment activities: UR, bill processing payment adjustments, and the process for resolving medical-necessity disputes. The chapter outlines potential changes to improve program oversight and streamline the medical-necessity dispute-resolution process.
- Chapter Six provides a framework for an ongoing system for monitoring access to medically appropriate care and discusses the potential for using the WCIS data for this purpose.
- Chapters Three through Six contain recommendations pertaining to the topics explored in the respective chapters. Chapter Seven summarizes those recommendations and discusses next steps for monitoring and evaluating the medical care provided under the WC program.

There are five electronic appendixes to the monograph that provide supplemental information on our analyses and findings:

- Appendix A provides an overview of the methods that were used to analyze the WCIS data in Chapters Three and Five.
- Appendixes B and C provide more-detailed information on the methods and findings pertaining to analyses of OSHPD data for inpatient hospital services and ambulatory surgery facility services, respectively, that are discussed in Chapter Three. The material in these appendixes was previously issued as several working papers.
- Appendix D provides more-detailed information and findings pertaining to analyses of OSHPD data for hospital emergency department services that are discussed in Chapter Four. The material in this appendix was also previously issued as a working paper.
- Appendix E presents a fuller discussion of models that use IMR organizations to resolve medical-necessity disputes. This topic is discussed in Chapter Five.

CHAPTER TWO

An Overview of Workers' Compensation Medical Expenditures

In this chapter, we begin with summary of the major provisions affecting medical care that is provided to injured workers and the implementation timeline. The purpose of this summary is to provide context for the overview that follows of the changes in how injured workers are utilizing the system, as reflected in expenditures on medical care. Our examination of changes in expenditures for WC medical care draws on published information both on California-specific trends in medical expenses and on benchmarking data. In Chapters Three through Five, we examine the impacts of specific provisions and provide a fuller explanation of the provisions in those chapters.

Summary of Reform Provisions Affecting Medical Treatment

The legislative provisions designed to control the cost of WC medical treatment were enacted in three successive revisions to the Labor Code:

- Assembly Bill (AB) 749 (Calderon, February 19, 2002)
- Senate Bill (SB) 228 (Alarcón, October 1, 2003)
- SB 899 (Poochigian, April 19, 2004).

Some policies initially established in AB 749 were revised by SB 228 and SB 899. Some policies were effective by date of injury, and others were effective by date of service. Following is a summary of the major policies that have affected the cost and use of medical services and their implementation dates.

- provisions directly affecting service utilization and medical-necessity determinations
  - *Elimination of the presumption that the findings of the treating physician are correct.* Initially, the presumption was eliminated effective with dates of injury occurring on or after January 1, 2003 (unless the worker had predesignated a personal physician prior to the injury). The presumption was completely repealed regardless of date of injury effective April 19, 2004, and replaced by the American College of Occupational and Environmental Medicine (ACOEM) guidelines.
  - *24-visit limits on chiropractic and therapy visits.* The limits apply to injuries occurring on or after January 1, 2004.
  - *Outpatient drugs.* Dispensing of generic equivalents is required unless a physician specifically provides for a nongeneric drug or the generic is not available. The provision

was initially applicable to pharmacies effective for services provided on or after January 1, 2003, and extended in 2004 to any person or entity that dispenses drugs.

- *UR.* The existing UR regulations were repealed effective January 1, 2004, and replaced by new requirements. DWC issued initial implementing regulations effective December 2004 and the enforcement regulations effective June 2007.

- provisions affecting injured worker choice of provider
  - *MPNs.* The provisions are effective for services furnished on or after January 1, 2005. Unless the employee has predesignated a primary-care physician, an employer with an approved medical network selects the treating physician for the first visit; thereafter, the employee may select a different physician within the network. Other than a change in eligibility for predesignation, there is no change in provider-choice policies if the employer does not have a medical network. The employer selects the treating physician for first 30 days (or 90–180 days in a health care organization); thereafter, the employee may select the treating physician.
  - *Predesignation of primary treating physician.* Effective April 2004, predesignation was eliminated for chiropractors and acupuncturists and the rules modified to allow an employee to predesignate a primary-care (allopathic and osteopathic) physician only if the employer provides nonoccupational health coverage. An injured worker may be treated by the predesignated physician from date of injury.

- provisions affecting provider payments
  - Allowances for physician and other practitioner services were reduced 5 percent (but not below the Medicare fee schedule) effective January 1, 2004. Administratively, the allowances for evaluation and management (E/M) services were increased effective for services furnished on or after February 15, 2007.
  - Allowances for other provider services were tied to Medicare-based fee schedules, with regular updates effective for services furnished on or after January 1, 2004. This was an expansion of the fee schedule to additional hospital inpatient and emergency facility services, ambulatory surgery facility services, and ambulance services and was intended to reduce expenditures for those services. For other services, including most inpatient hospital services and durable medical equipment (DME) and supplies, this provision updated the fee schedules and resulted in annual updates in the allowances that have increased expenditures for those services over time.
  - Allowances for outpatient drugs and other pharmaceutical products were based on 100 percent of the Medi-Cal fee schedule effective January 1, 2004, and were intended to reduce pharmaceutical expenditures.

Trends in Total Expenditures for Medical Care

During the pre-2004 period, medical-care expenditures had been increasing twice as fast as indemnity payments for temporary and permanent disability. Medical-care expenditures dropped 21 percent from 2003 to 2005 when the reform provisions were first implemented, then remained flat for several years but increased 10.6 percent from 2007 to 2009 (Figure 2.1). Because indemnity benefits also decreased over the postreform period, medical expenditures increased from 51 percent to 60 percent of estimated system-wide calendar year paid losses from 2003 to 2009.

Figure 2.1
California Workers' System-Wide Estimated Costs: 2000–2009 Medical and Indemnity Calendar Year Paid Benefits

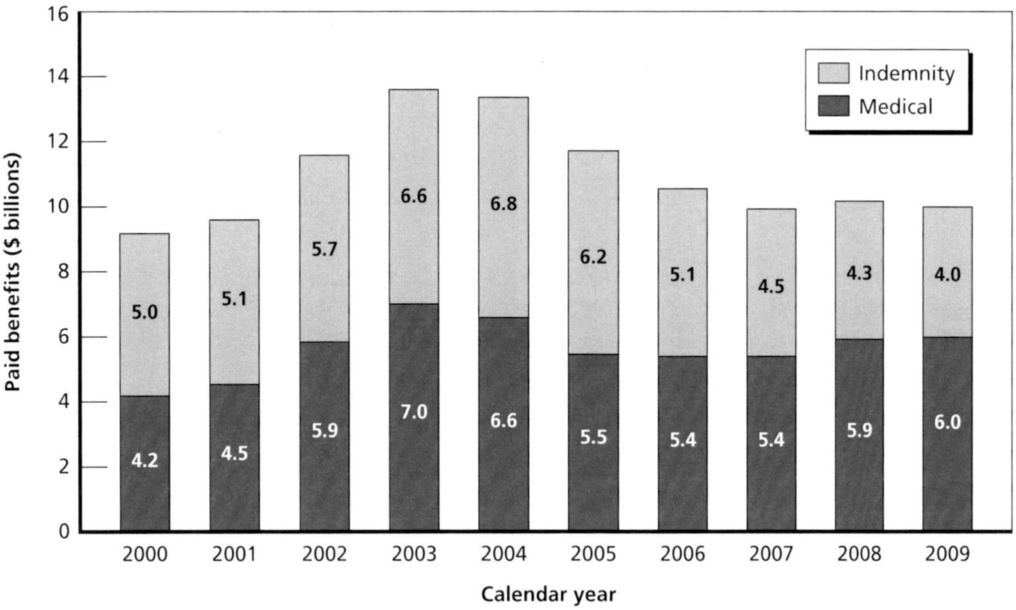

SOURCE: CHSWC, 2010b. WCIRB data on insurer costs were adjusted by a factor of 1.43 to estimate system-wide costs for insurers and self-insured employers.
RAND MG1144-2.1

Figure 2.1 shows the overall rate of growth in WC annual expenditures. The change in aggregate expenditures is affected not only by implementation of the reform provisions but also by significant reductions in the number of WC claims since 2004. Since it is unlikely that the reduction in the number of new WC claims is related to implementation of the reform provisions, per-claim measures of medical expenses might be more relevant than the measures of aggregate expenditures. The change in ultimate medical loss per indemnity claim (total incurred or expected medical costs over the life of the claim that involved disability payments) is an important metric that has direct implications for the pure premium rate for WC insurers (Figure 2.2). Relative to Figure 2.1, the cost reductions are less marked for two reasons. First, the overall annual expenses reflect the decline in the number of claims, as well as the reform provisions, while the average ultimate loss per claim is affected only by the reform provisions. Second, the ultimate losses for pre-2004 accident years have been lowered to account for the estimated effects that the reform provisions have on care that will be provided in the postreform period on open claims for that accident year. The ultimate medical loss per indemnity claim reached its lowest level in AY 2004 and had an annual growth rate of 8.6 percent between AYs 2004 and 2010.

Another key performance measure is how WC benefit expenditures compare to WC programs in other states. According to NASI, benefits under California's WC program per $100 covered payroll were considerably higher in 2004 at the outset of the reform provisions than in the rest of the United States (including both state and federal WC programs) and remain higher despite implementation of the reforms (Figure 2.3). In 2008, California's total benefits per $100 were $1.21, compared with $0.93 for the rest of the country. With respect to medical

Figure 2.2
Estimated Ultimate Total Loss per Insured Indemnity Claim as of December 31, 2010

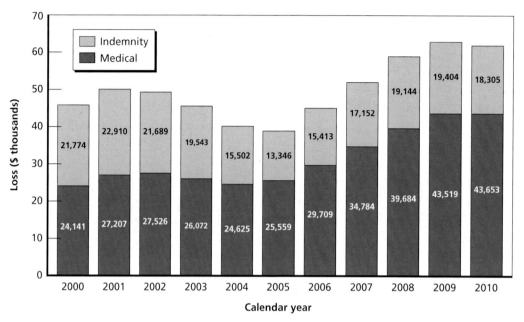

SOURCE: WCIRB, 2011.

RAND *MG1144-2.2*

Figure 2.3
California Workers' Compensation Expenses per $100 Payroll Compared with Workers' Compensation Programs in the Rest of the United States, 2004–2008

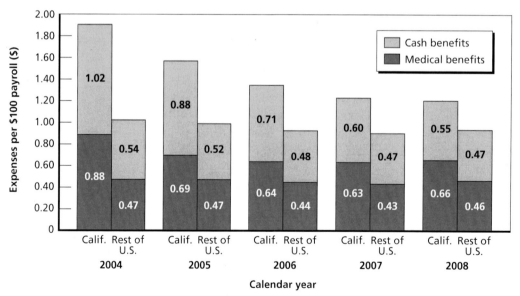

SOURCES: Sengupta, Reno, and Burton, 2008, 2010; personal communication with NASI staff to obtain medical expenses exclusive of medical cost-containment expenses for 2004–2005.

NOTE: Medical benefits do not include medical cost-containment expenses.

RAND *MG1144-2.3*

benefits (exclusive of medical cost-containment expenses), benefits per $100 of covered payroll in the rest of the United States have remained relatively steady over the 2000–2008 period and were estimated at $0.46 in 2008. In contrast, medical benefits per $100 of covered payroll in California decreased from a high of $0.88 in 2004, when the reforms were implemented, to a low of $0.63 in 2007 before rising to $0.66 per $100 of covered payroll in 2008, about 43 percent higher than the rest of the United States.

In understanding the growth of WC medical costs, it is also helpful to compare the increases in WC medical expenses to increases in group health premiums and other measures of medical cost growth. For WC, Figure 2.4 shows, by accident year, the cumulative growth in the average first 12 months of medical expenses per indemnity claim for the sample of payers in the CWCI database. The California HealthCare Foundation (CHCF) conducts an annual survey of employer health benefits. Premium increases under employer health plans are a benchmark, albeit an imperfect one, for the WC program. Changes in the average premium for all employer health plans are affected by changes in product mix, as well as by premium increases.[1] To hold the product mix constant in measuring premium changes, the premium across all years is for individual coverage in a preferred-provider organization (PPO) plan and includes both employee and employer contributions. Some employers are constraining the rate of growth in premiums by reducing benefits and increasing employee cost-sharing. Because WC covers all medical care for work-related injuries and illnesses without cost-sharing, a better comparison would include changes in the value of the employee cost-sharing and out-of-pocket expenses for noncovered care. However, we were unable to identify a source of information that would enable us to add these changes to the comparison. The other measures in Figure 2.4 are the cumulative growth in overall California inflation and in the medical component of the Consumer Price Index (CPI) for all urban populations. For each indicator, the 2002 value is assigned an index value of 100.

As seen in Figure 2.4, the cumulative increases in both the average WC medical expenses per indemnity claim (40.4 percent) and the average monthly premium for individual PPO coverage (65.5 percent) between 2002 and 2009 outpaced the 19.7-percent and 33.4-percent increases in overall California inflation and the medical CPI, respectively. The difference between the average expense and premium measures and the price-inflation measures is largely attributable to changes in the volume and intensity of medical services but might also reflect changes in administrative costs, benefit design, and employee demographics. Without the reform provisions, the rate of increase over the period is likely to have been at least as great as the rate of increase in the PPO premium over the period. Although this suggests that expenditure levels are lower than what they would have been in the absence of the reform provisions, a concern is that WC medical expenses have increased 13.1 percent annually, compared with a 7.2-percent average increase in the PPO premium since 2005, when average WC expenses per indemnity claim were at their lowest point. This higher rate of increase prompts concerns about whether further policy changes are needed to create better incentives for the efficient delivery of high-quality care under California's WC program.

Aggregate expenditures for WC medical care dropped 21 percent from 2003 to 2005 when the reform provisions were first implemented, then remained flat for several years. But

---

[1] For example, the CHCF survey of 2009 benefits found that the average premium increase for firms that offered the same health plans in 2009 and 2010 was 7.5 percent, compared with 0.7 percent when firms that changed plans or had workers who switched plans are included (CHCF, 2010).

Figure 2.4
Cumulative Growth in Paid Medical Expenses per Indemnity Claim at 12 Months, Compared with Rates of Growth in California Employer Health Premium for Individual Preferred-Provider Organization Coverage, Overall California Inflation and the Medical Consumer Price Index, 2002–2009

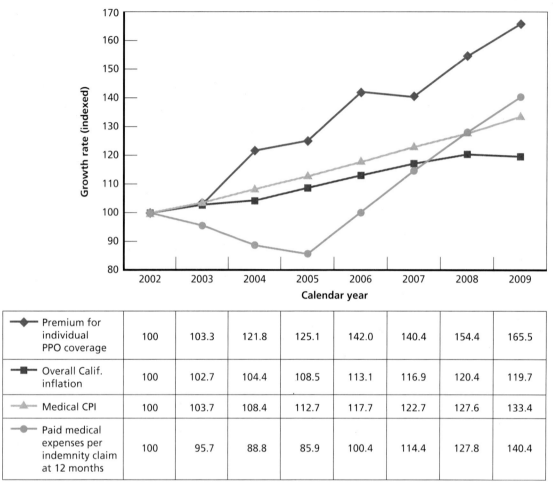

	2002	2003	2004	2005	2006	2007	2008	2009
Premium for individual PPO coverage	100	103.3	121.8	125.1	142.0	140.4	154.4	165.5
Overall Calif. inflation	100	102.7	104.4	108.5	113.1	116.9	120.4	119.7
Medical CPI	100	103.7	108.4	112.7	117.7	122.7	127.6	133.4
Paid medical expenses per indemnity claim at 12 months	100	95.7	88.8	85.9	100.4	114.4	127.8	140.4

SOURCES: CHCF, 2005, 2006b, 2007, 2008, 2009, 2010; Kaiser Family Foundation, undated; Bureau of Labor Statistics (BLS), undated; Swedlow and Ireland, 2008.
NOTE: Index value for 2002 = 100.
RAND MG1144-2.4

from 2007 to 2009, they increased sharply. The flatness observed in total medical expenses is largely attributable to the declining claim volume. The rising costs starting in 2007 are attributed not so much to the delivery of actual medical services as to the administrative costs associated with medical benefits, such as medical cost-containment and medical-legal expenses.

Medical Expenditure Trends, by Payment Category

Figure 2.5 summarizes the changes in annual medical expenses over the period 2002–2009 based on WCIRB data on insurer payments for medical costs adjusted to reflect system-wide payments (payments made by both insurers and self-insured employers). Expenses are cat-

Figure 2.5
Distribution of System-Wide Workers' Compensation Medical Expenses, by Payee Category, 2002–2009

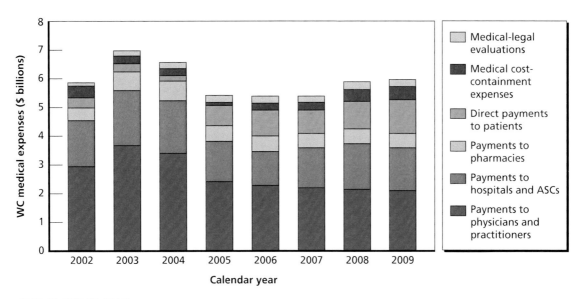

SOURCE: CHSWC, 2010b.

NOTE: ASC = ambulatory surgical center. WCIRB data on insurer costs were adjusted by a factor of 1.43 to estimate system-wide costs.

RAND *MG1144-2.5*

egorized by the entity that received the payments (as opposed to the type of service that was provided). For example, payments for physician-dispensed drugs are included in the physician payment category. The largest category of expenses is for payments to physicians and other practitioners, followed by that for payments to hospitals. The increase in total spending between 2008 and 2009 is attributable to apparent increases in medical cost-containment expenses and direct payments to patients. In part, this is the result of more-detailed reporting of expenses into payee categories (WCIRB, 2010b). The medical cost-containment expenses depicted in Figure 2.5 include both administrative costs (e.g., MPN license fees) and some direct patient-care costs (e.g., case management). As discussed in Chapter Five, current WCIRB policy now requires reporting medical cost expenses separately from other medical expenses. Direct payments to patients are mostly lump-sum settlements of claims but also include payments for transportation related to medical care.

Figure 2.5 indicates that expenses for actual medical care have been rising less rapidly than expenses related to administration of the medical benefit, such as medical cost-containment expenses and medical-legal expenses. Aggregate payments to hospitals, physicians, and pharmacies remained below prereform (2003) levels in 2009, while medical cost-containment expenses doubled between 2004 and 2009. Medical-legal expenses fluctuated slightly over the period, but the payment levels in 2009 were comparable to 2004 levels.

Summary of Findings

Our examination of changes in annual medical expenditures for WC medical care show the following:

- Annual paid medical losses fell sharply after implementation of the reform provisions but have been rising since 2008.
- Reduced payments to providers were the major contributing factor to the initial reductions in annual paid losses. Subsequently, expenses for actual medical care have been rising less rapidly than expenses related to administration of the medical benefit, such as medical cost-containment expenses, medical-legal expenses, and direct payments to workers.
- Annual paid medical losses remain significantly lower than they would have been in the absence of the reform provisions but continue to be higher than they are for WC programs in other states.

These losses have been affected not only by the medical reform provisions but also significant reductions in the number of WC claims. Since it is unlikely that the reduction in the number of new WC claims is related to implementation of the reform provisions, per-claim measures of medical expenses might be more relevant than the measures of aggregate expenditures. For insured indemnity claims, the average paid losses per claim at 12 months valuation were at their lowest level in 2005 and subsequently have been increasing 13.1 percent annually. Further research is needed to determine whether the decline in WC claims has affected the severity of injuries and the cost trends.

CHAPTER THREE

Payments for Medical Services Provided to Injured Workers

This chapter begins with an overview of the distribution of payments for medical services. We then focus on the major types of medical services provided to injured workers: physician and other practitioner services, inpatient hospital services, ambulatory surgery facility services and outpatient drugs and other pharmaceuticals. For each type of service, we summarize the most-important reform provisions, examine changes in the use and cost of services, and highlight selected issues for which additional policy changes might improve the quality and efficiency of medical services.

Distribution of Payments for Medical Services

In Figure 3.1, we show the distribution of payments to providers in 2007. The largest percentage of payments was to physicians, nearly $3.2 billion, or 41 percent of total payments. Payments to hospitals represented just under $2 billion, or approximately one-quarter of all payments. This includes payments for inpatient and outpatient services, as well as payments to ASCs. Payments to pharmacies comprised about 9 percent ($710 million). Approximately $1.2 billion in payments were made directly to patients. Medical-legal payments to physicians and medical cost-containment expenses combined represented roughly 9 percent of total payments. Not shown in Figure 3.2 is approximately $12 million in capitation payments made to medical groups.

We used the 2007 WCIS data to further breakdown the distribution of payments to providers. The methods we used for the analyses of WCIS data are described in Appendix A. Medical-payment data are reported separately for institutional providers, such as hospitals and ASCs, and noninstitutional providers, such as physicians and other practitioners, pharmacies, and DME providers. Approximately 69 percent of total payments to institutional providers were to acute-care hospitals, while 27 percent of payments were billed by ASCs (Figure 3.2). Less than 5 percent of institutional payments were paid to other hospitals, including psychiatric and rehabilitation hospitals.

With respect to noninstitutional providers, just over three-fourths of payments went to physicians, while 20 percent of payments were made to nonphysician providers. In Figure 3.3, we show the WCIS distribution of payments to noninstitutional providers by type of service (in contrast to the WCRIB data, which showed the distribution by broad payee category). As explained in Appendix A, we used the reported procedure codes to define the type of service. The largest share of payments was for physician services, including E/M visits (16 percent of payments), surgery (10 percent), and hospitalist services (hospital-based physician services to

**Figure 3.1
Distribution of Estimated System-Wide Workers' Compensation Paid
Medical Expenses in 2007 by Payee Category ($ millions)**

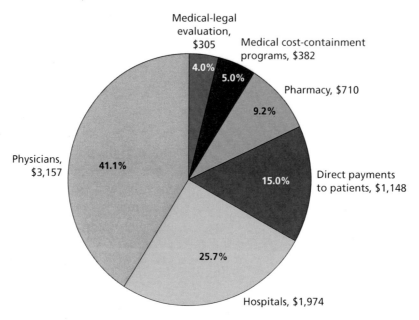

SOURCE: CHSWC, 2010b.

NOTE: WCIRB data on insurer costs were adjusted by a factor of 1.43 to estimate
system-wide costs. Hospitals include ASCs.

RAND *MG1144-3.1*

**Figure 3.2
Distribution of Payments to Institutional Providers in 2007**

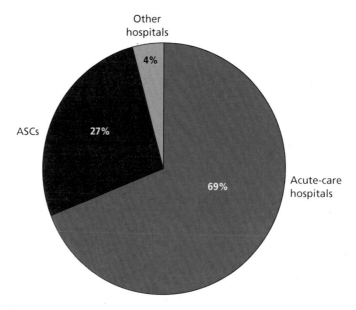

SOURCE: RAND analysis of WCIS 2007 data.

RAND *MG1144-3.2*

Figure 3.3
Distribution of Workers' Compensation Payments to Noninstitutional Providers, by Type of Service, 2007

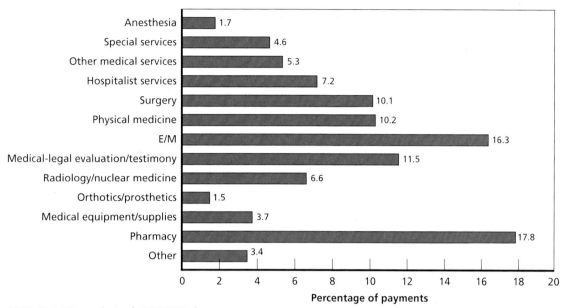

SOURCE: RAND analysis of WCIS 2007 data.

RAND *MG1144-3.3*

inpatients) (7 percent). Physical medicine accounted for 10 percent of total payments to non-institutional providers. Nearly 18 percent of payments were made for outpatient drugs and other pharmaceutical products to pharmacies and physicians. Medical-legal evaluations and testimony comprised 11 percent of payments to noninstitutional providers.

Figure 3.4 displays the distribution of payments by place of service, including payments to both institutional and noninstitutional providers. The distribution is based on total WCIS-reported payments for all services provided in each setting, including professional services, facility fees, outpatient drugs, and medical equipment and supplies. The majority of payments were for services provided to WC patients in office settings or independent clinics (63 percent), followed by inpatient settings (16 percent), and hospital outpatient settings or ASCs (15 percent). We were unable to fully distinguish care rendered in hospital outpatient settings from care delivered in ASCs, because of possible inaccuracies in the use of place of service codes. About 3.4 percent of total spending was devoted to services patients received in their home. Nearly half of these services were for medical equipment and supplies (45 percent), followed by orthotics and prosthetics (11 percent). Due to lack of procedure codes, using our taxonomy, we were not able to classify 26 percent of the services delivered in a patient's home. The remaining 2.2 percent of services were provided in a range of settings, including skilled-nursing facilities (0.7 percent) and hospital emergency departments (EDs) (0.5 percent).

Physician and Other Practitioner Services

In this section, we provide an overview of the major reform provisions affecting the use and costs of services provided by physicians and other practitioners. We then provide information

Figure 3.4
Distribution of Workers' Compensation Medical Payments, by Place of Service, 2007

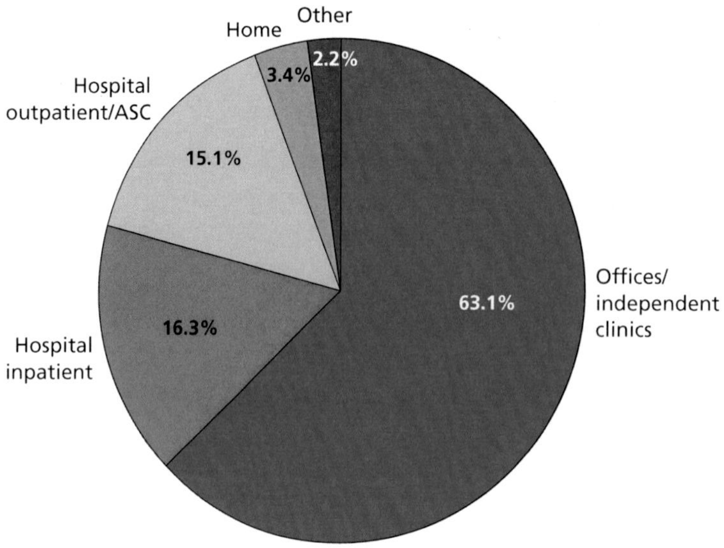

SOURCE: RAND analysis of WCIS 2007 data.
RAND *MG1144-3.4*

on the trends in aggregate payments to these providers, describe changes in service use, and conclude with a discussion of the fee-schedule allowances for services.

We synthesized information from several sources to assess the reforms' impact on the use and costs of physician and other practitioner services. The interviews that we conducted in 2006–2007 with knowledgeable individuals involved in the WC medical-treatment system identified areas of concern during the initial implementation of the reforms. We drew on published reports from the WCIRB, WCRI, and CWCI to examine utilization and cost trends and to benchmark service utilization to other states.

Key Reform Provisions Affecting Service Use and Costs

Three key reform provisions directly affected the provision of physician and other practitioner services to injured workers: the MTUS, caps on physical therapy and chiropractic manipulation, and changes in the OMFS allowances for physician and practitioner services. The MTUS was established to provide a formal set of evidence-based practice guidelines that replace the presumption accorded the primary treating physician. The MTUS is presumptively correct on the scope and duration of care that is reasonably required to cure or relieve the effects of the injury. The guidelines are rebuttable by a preponderance of scientific evidence establishing that a variance from the guidelines is reasonably required. For injuries not covered by the designated guidelines, treatment is to be in accordance with other evidence based medical-treatment guidelines generally recognized by the community.

Effective for services provided on or after April 1, 2004, the medical guidelines established by ACOEM were implemented by statute as the interim MTUS until DWC adopted other guidelines. DWC incorporated the ACOEM guidelines into its MTUS effective in June 15, 2007, and added guidelines for acupuncture. Additional guidelines for chronic pain (adapted from the Work Loss Data Institute's *Official Disability Guidelines*) and postsurgical physical medicine treatment were added effective July 18, 2009 (California Department of Industrial Relations, undated [a]). A process was established for augmenting and updating the guidelines using a medical evidence evaluation advisory committee.

The second key reform established a limit of 24 chiropractic, occupational, and physical therapy visits each, unless the cap is waived by a claim administrator. The cap is applied independent of the MTUS. As discussed later in this section, California's use of these services was much higher than in other states.

The third key reform was changes in the OMFS for physician and other practitioner services. The reform provisions placed most services on Medicare-based fee schedules with regular updates. An exception was the OMFS for physician and practitioner services. Effective January 1, 2004, allowances for services that exceed the Medicare fee schedule were reduced 5 percent (but not below Medicare rates), and the remaining services are frozen until the DWC AD establishes a new fee schedule for physician and practitioner services. Administratively, the OMFS allowances for some E/M services were increased in 2007 to Medicare payment levels.

Common Themes from 2006–2007 Interviews

Among most interviewees, there was some consensus that the guidelines were well-designed for the acute conditions that they addressed but that they were deficient for not addressing chronic pain, alternative therapies, and use of pharmaceuticals, including for indications not approved by the U.S. Food and Drug Administration (FDA). The MTUS revisions to include acupuncture and chronic pain have largely addressed these concerns. However, two other concerns that were raised in the interviews might remain applicable. First, concerns were often expressed not with the guidelines per se but that they were being applied too stringently during UR and that insufficient attention was paid to the individual patient's condition that might warrant deviation from the guidelines. UR processes are subject to routine investigations by DWC, but, as discussed in Chapter Five, these investigations focus on procedural issues rather than on the quality of the medical decisions. Further analysis of this issue—which would require independent medical review of UR decisions—is warranted. Second, there were some concerns that the Labor Code requirement that any medical guidelines to be adopted must be evidence based, nationally recognized, and peer reviewed precluded establishing needed guidelines for therapies that do not have a robust evidence base. This issue has most recently arisen with respect to compound drugs and medical foods, for which there is a limited evidence base on which to establish guidelines. Medical-necessity disputes over the compound drug and medical food products revolve around whether the products should be covered only if there is evidence supporting that they are medically appropriate or whether they should be covered *unless* there is evidence that they are not safe and effective.

Considerable concern was also voiced over the therapy caps. Although interviewees generally indicated that the caps would help reduce the amount of medically unnecessary care, even to the point of driving some ineffective and potentially wasteful clinics out of business, some expressed concern over delays or denials in care to patients needing more than the allotted visits and suggested that, when conservative care, such as therapy, is denied, physicians might turn to more-aggressive care for their patients. The interviewees were confident that at least some payers were allowing for waivers of caps when medically necessary (typically, following surgery) but noted that the waivers were generally for physical therapy but not chiropractic care. Since the time the interviews were conducted, DWC has incorporated postsurgical therapy treatment guidelines into the MTUS, which should have reduced some of the treatment delays caused by the UR process.

The physician fee schedule was not a commonly raised issue during the interviews. The practice of payers requiring providers to accept discounted fees in return for participation in the medical provider networks was a commonly raised concern that is addressed in Chapter Four.

Changes in Aggregate Payments

As discussed in Chapter Two, physician and other practitioner services were most affected by the changes in medical-treatment policies. Estimated system-wide payments for these services declined from a high of $3.7 billion in 2003 to $2.1 billion in 2009. The impact has varied across different specialties (Table 3.1). In 2003, chiropractors received 21.6 percent of WC medical payments to physicians, compared with 5.2 percent of payments in 2009, an estimated 81-percent reduction that reflects the imposition of the 24-visit-per-injury limitation and the impact of the ACOEM guidelines. The impact that these changes had on physical therapists was not as great: Their payments fell 34 percent, compared with an overall 43-percent reduction in payments to all physicians and practitioners. Among primary-care specialties, payments increased for general and family practice (23 percent) and occupational medicine specialties (25 percent). Other specialties that experienced increases over the period included orthopedic surgery (19 percent), radiology (28 percent), physical medicine (57 percent), anesthesiology (40 percent) and psychiatry (34 percent). Payments fell about 50 percent for internal medicine subspecialties, general surgery, and acupuncture.

Service Utilization and Intensity

Changes in total payments are affected by changes in the number of WC claims, the services per claim, and the price per service. WCRI provides benchmarking information on medical expenditures for WC claims for 15 states (including California) that can be used to explain the changes in service use and intensity on a per-claim basis and to identify those areas in which California's medical prices or utilization are out of line with the 15-state comparison group. The latest available data are for claims with dates of injury from October 1, 2006, through September 30, 2007, valued as of April 1, 2008, (2007 claims at an average of 12 months). Table 3.2 summarizes selected WCRI benchmarking indices for physician and other practitioner services. Payments exclude any payments to hospitals associated with the services (e.g., the facility fees for major surgery). WCRI reports the average payment per user for each category based on the sum of the payments for the category divided by the number of claims with services in that category. We derived the average payment per claim for each service category from the WCRI data by multiplying the average payment per user by the percentage of claims with services in that category. The price index is for calendar year 2007. The price index measures the price of a fixed basket of services relative to the median for the 15 states. The median price is assigned an index value of 100, so that California's index value of 96 for nonhospital services means that fees for these services were 4 percent lower than the median for the comparison group. Except for neurologic and neuromuscular testing (price index = 122), the price index for each type of service is at or below 100.

The utilization index captures the volume (number of visits per claim) and intensity (resources required for the mix of services provided during the visits). California's overall index for nonhospital services is 96, indicating that, for the 2007–2008 claims, utilization (volume

Table 3.1
Change in System-Wide Medical Payments to Physicians and Other Practitioners, 2003–2009

Practice Type	Total Medical Payments ($ 000s)		% Change	% of Classified Physician Costs	
Specialty	2003	2009	2003–2009	2003	2009
Chiropractor	504,175	93,920	–81	21.6	5.2
Clinics	391,892	325,151	–17	16.8	18.2
General and family practice	315,568	388,108	23	13.5	21.7
Physical therapy	276,672	182,484	–34	11.8	10.2
Orthopedic surgery	154,115	183,187	19	6.6	10.2
General surgery	114,486	56,802	–50	4.9	3.2
Radiology	77,057	98,721	28	3.3	5.5
Physical medicine: MDs	74,856	117,249	57	3.2	6.6
Internal medicine	59,078	28,722	–51	2.5	1.6
Emergency	46,235	14,094	–70	2.0	0.8
Anesthesiology	39,997	55,893	40	1.7	3.1
Psychologist	37,061	33,689	–9	1.6	1.9
Occupational medicine	35,960	45,068	25	1.5	2.5
Acupuncture	33,392	17,011	–49	1.4	1.0
Osteopaths	27,153	20,302	–25	1.2	1.1
Neurology	25,318	25,388	0	1.1	1.4
Psychiatry	24,952	33,319	34	1.1	1.9
Other	100,542	70,563	–30	4.3	4.0
Total classified payments to physicians and other practitioners	2,338,508	1,789,672	–23		
Unknown or not otherwise classified	1,330,891	312,728	–77		
Total payments to physicians and other practitioners	3,669,399	2,102,400	–43		

SOURCES: WCIRB, 2004, 2010b.

and intensity) is slightly below the 15-state median. The 2007–2008 utilization index is markedly below the 2002–2003 utilization index value of 152.[1]

California's substantially higher use of E/M services than that of other states has continued in the postreform period with approximately the same number of visits per claim as prereform. For the 2007–2008 claims, there were 9.2 visits, compared with the median of 5.9 for the comparison group. There were also slightly more services per visit (1.1 versus 1.02), but the

---

[1] The change in index values could also be affected by a change in the composition of the comparison group. There were 13 states in the 2002–2003 comparison group: California, Connecticut, Florida, Illinois, Indiana, Louisiana, Massachusetts, North Carolina, Pennsylvania, Tennessee, Texas, and Wisconsin. For the 2007–2008 comparison group, Connecticut was dropped and Iowa and Maryland were added.

Table 3.2
Summary of Workers Compensation Research Institute Measures for Nonhospital Services Provided for Claims with More Than Seven Days Lost Work, 2002–2003 and 2007–2008

Type of Health Care Service	2007–2008 Claims[a]				2002–2003 Claims: Utilization Index[b]
	Average Payment per Claim ($)	Average Payment per User *$(	Price Index	Utilization Index	
E/M	815	849	81	185	192
Major radiology	295	757	87	97	104
Minor radiology	120	160	100	108	116
Major surgery	625	2,500	100	105	105
Surgical treatment	220	458	66	91	118
Neurologic/ neuromuscular testing	157	653	122	87	111
Physical medicine	699	1,059	92	61	160
All nonhospital services			96	102	152

SOURCES: WCRI, 2005; Coomer et al., 2010.

[a] Claims arising between October 1, 2006, and September 30, 2007, valued as of April 1, 2008. Price index for calendar year 2007.

[b] Claims arising between October 1, 2001, and September 30, 2002, valued as of April 1, 2003.

visits were also 20 percent more resource-intensive than in other states. A higher percentage of visits are billed as extended or comprehensive visits than in the comparison group. The overall result is that the average payment per claim for E/M services is in the top third of the 15 states despite having the lowest price index.

The utilization index for major surgery remained unchanged between the 2002–2003 and 2007–2008 claims. The utilization indices for all other services declined over the period, with a marked drop in the physical medicine utilization index from 160 to 61. The average physical medicine payment per claim ($1,059) is in the bottom third of the comparison group. The average payment for minor surgical procedures is also in the bottom third of the comparison group, largely because of the low fees for the services relative to the comparison group.

The utilization index value for neurologic and neuromuscular testing dropped from 111 to 87; however, about the same percentage of claims as before involve these services (data not shown). In comparison with the 15-state median for the 2007–2008 claims, a higher percentage of claims use these services (24 percent versus 11 percent), and there are more visits per claim (1.8 versus 1.3), but the visits have 11 percent lower resource intensity.

The WCRI benchmarking data further confirm the significant impact that the reform provisions have on chiropractic care (Table 3.3). The percentage of claims with chiropractic care fell from 19 percent to 11 percent between the 2002–2003 claims and 2007–2008 claims, and the number of visits per claim is about 25 percent of prereform levels (10.6 versus 39.5). The utilization index is now 88 (compared to a prereform level of 260).

Table 3.3
Summary of Workers Compensation Research Institute Measures for Chiropractic Services Provided for Claims with More Than Seven Days Lost Work, 2002–2003 and 2007–2008

Measure	2007–2008 Claims[a]	2002–2003 Claims[b]
Percentage of claims with chiropractic care	11	19
Number of visits per claim	10.6	39.5
Average payment per claim ($)	120	706
Average payment per user ($)	1,091	3,717
Utilization index	88	260

SOURCES: WCRI, 2005; Coomer et al., 2010.

[a] Claims arising between October 1, 2006, and September 30, 2007, valued as of April 1, 2008. Price index for calendar year 2007.

[b] Claims arising between October 1, 2001, and September 30, 2002, valued as of April 1, 2003.

The MTUS guidelines are fairly specific with particular treatment modalities but more general with respect to follow-up visits.[2] Thus, it is not surprising that the imaging and neuromuscular services have been affected more than E/M visits. What is interesting, however, is how little impact the MTUS seem to have had on major surgical procedures. About the same percentage of 2007–2008 claims had major surgery as in 2002–2003 (25 percent versus 27 percent). An expectation was that the ACOEM guideline emphasis on conservative care would reduce the incidence of major surgery. Further investigation of this issue is warranted for specific conditions.

Official Medical Fee Schedule Allowances

As noted earlier, the reform provisions left the current OMFS for physician and practitioner services in place (with up to a 5-percent reduction) until the DWC AD issues a new fee schedule. Administratively, the AD raised the allowances for E/M services to Medicare levels, which had the effect of increasing payments for office visits by nearly 14 percent (Yang, Coomer, Landes, et al., 2010) and overall payments for physician services approximately 2.2 percent (Lewin Group, 2010). Other than this change, the OMFS for physician and practitioner services has not been updated for many years. The OMFS primarily uses the 1997 Current Procedural Terminology (CPT) codes to describe most services with some WC-specific codes and 1994 CPT codes for anesthesia and physical medicine. Updated procedure codes are needed to expand the OMFS to cover new (and often high-cost) procedures and reduce disputes concerning a reasonable fee for those services. It would bring WC into compliance with the coding system used by Medicare and private payers. This would eliminate the need for nonoccupational health providers to maintain two coding systems and enable better benchmarking with other health plans.

A second shortcoming to the OMFS is that current fee schedule is based on historical, charge-based relative values that undervalue primary-care services relative to other services. Even with the 2007 increase in payments for E/M services, they are likely to be undervalued. The OMFS does not explicitly pay for many work-related services that medical providers offer

---

[2] The general guideline is that physician follow-up might occur every four to seven days when the patient is off work and once every week or two if the patient is working (ACOEM, 2004).

to injured workers, such as care coordination and consultations with employers on return-to-work issues. A Lewin Group study on physician effort with injured workers concluded that E/M services provided to injured workers require about 28 percent more effort than services to Medicare patients (Dobson et al., 2003). One reason the procedure-oriented services are over-valued is that historical, charge-based relative values do not reflect the impact of technology diffusion lowering the cost of new procedures over time.

A third shortcoming to the OMFS is that overall payment levels are low relative to other services paid under the California WC system. Except for pharmaceuticals that are paid based on the Medi-Cal fee schedule, the OMFS allowances for other services are based on 120 per-cent of what would be allowed under Medicare for an allowable service. In the aggregate, estimated OMFS allowances for physician and practitioner services are about 1.11 times the Medicare fee-schedule levels (Lewin Group, 2010).[3] Nationally, Medicare payments to physi-cians are about 80 percent of private-payer levels (Medicare Payment Advisory Commission [MedPAC], 2011a), although there is substantial difference both across and within geographic areas (MedPAC, 2011b). Because having high-quality physicians is fundamental to increasing the value of medical care provided under the WC system, paying less for physician services than for other services is short-sighted.

DWC has proposed a new Medicare-based fee schedule for physician and other prac-titioner services, which sets rates based on the relative resources (physician time and effort, practice expenses, and malpractice insurance costs) required to provide services (California Department of Industrial Relations, undated [b]). By aligning payments with the costs of care, neutral incentives are created to provide appropriate care. If payments are substantially higher than costs, providers have an incentive to provide marginal or unnecessary care or to determine the venue for treatment based on financial considerations rather than on the needs of the patient. If payments are substantially lower than costs, access to medically necessary care can be adversely affected. A resource-based fee schedule also has the potential to improve OMFS payment equity across physician specialties, particularly if a single conversion factor is adopted that would increase payments for primary care relative to other services. With respect to E/M services, further rate increases are appropriate under a resource-based relative-value fee schedule, but, at a minimum, they should be accompanied by the adoption of Medicare's documentation requirements for E/M visits (CMS, 2010b). As discussed earlier, the WCRI benchmarking data indicate that there is substantially higher use of E/M services in California than in other states (Yang, Coomer, Landes, et al., 2010). Alternatively, it might be more effec-tive to create payments for specific work-related activities in lieu of additional, across-the-board increases for E/M services (Wynn and Sorbero, 2008).

Inpatient Hospital Services

In this section, we first provide summary of the major reform provisions affecting the use and costs of inpatient hospital services—namely, changes in the OMFS allowances for inpatient stays. We then provide an overview of the trends in inpatient hospital stays for WC patients and examine the adequacy of payments under the OMFS. We conclude by focusing on three

---

[3]   The 1.11 estimate is based on the CWCI sample claims that the Lewin Group used in the modeling. The estimate was 1.18 using the WCRI weights for service mix.

issues for which additional fee-schedule changes might be appropriate: the pass-through for the costs of hardware implanted during spinal surgery, the inflationary impact of recent changes in the patient classification system, and the continued exemption of specialty hospitals from the OMFS.

To assess the impact that the OMFS changes could have on the use and costs of inpatient care provided to WC patients, we used inpatient discharge data from OSHPD. A description of our methodology and more-detailed findings on changes in the volume and distribution of inpatient stays, changes in payments, and an assessment of the adequacy of payments compared with estimated costs are in Appendix B.

Description of the Official Medical Fee Schedule Provisions

The OMFS for inpatient care provided by acute-care hospitals is adapted from the Medicare payment system for these services. A predetermined maximum allowable fee is established for each admission based on the diagnosis-related group (DRG) to which the patient is assigned. The DRG assignment takes into account such factors as the patient's principal diagnosis, comorbidities and complications, and surgical procedures. Each DRG has a relative weight reflecting the average resources or costs for Medicare patients assigned to that DRG relative to Medicare patients in other DRGs. The OMFS standard allowance for a discharge is determined as the product of a facility-specific composite rate times the DRG relative weight times 1.20.[4] Additional allowances are made for discharges with atypically high costs and for the cost of hardware (implanted devices and instrumentation) used in complex spinal surgery. Effective December 2007, the OMFS update incorporated Medicare severity DRG (MS-DRG)–adjusted rates that are designed to improve payment accuracy.

The OMFS for inpatient hospital services has been based on the Medicare fee schedule since 1999; however, regular updates did not occur until the provisions of SB 228 (2003) were implemented effective January 1, 2004. The rates that were updated January 1, 2004, had been in effect for two years (and had been based on 120 percent of the Medicare rates in effect at that time). Updating to the current Medicare rates and providing for annual updates increases aggregate payments but provides for more-equitable payments. SB 228 provisions related to inpatient hospital services included the following:

- Eliminating existing exemptions for certain types of cases: psychiatric and rehabilitation care unless provided in a special unit or specialty hospital, burn and trauma care, tracheostomy, and life-threatening inpatient care provided by Level I and II trauma hospitals. The provision reduced expenditures for these services.
- Eliminating an adjustment factor that applied to certain types of cases to either increase or decrease the payment relative to 120 percent of what Medicare would pay for the discharge. This provision had the effect of increasing payments for some services and reducing it for others.

---

[4] The composite rate is a hospital-specific rate based on the Medicare standard payment rate adjusted for geographic differences in wages and, if applicable, the hospital's additional payments for teaching and for serving a disproportionate share of low-income patients.

Labor Code Section 5307.1(a) specifies that the maximum allowable fees shall not exceed 120 percent of the estimated aggregate fees allowed under the Medicare payment system. In establishing the OMFS, the AD adopted a 1.20 multiplier so that aggregate payments will approximate 120 percent of the Medicare allowable payments for comparable services.

- Limiting a pass-through for the costs of hardware (implanted devices and instrumentation) used during any back and neck surgeries to only hardware used during spinal surgeries. Previously, the pass-through also applied to other back and neck procedures, so that the effect of the change was to reduce expenditures.
- Effective January 1, 2005, eliminating the exemption from Medicare-based fee schedules for hospitals that are not paid under the Medicare payment system for acute-care hospitals. As discussed later in this section, this provision has not yet been implemented, and specialty hospitals, including psychiatric and rehabilitation facilities, remain exempt from the OMFS.

Overview of Workers' Compensation Discharges from Acute-Care Hospitals and Estimated Payments

Overall, average payments per discharge increased nearly 34 percent between 2003 and 2008, about two-thirds of which was attributable to case-mix changes and one-third of which was attributable to inflation and other rate changes.

Table 3.4 provides summary information on acute-care hospital inpatient stays. In 2008, these stays accounted for 94 percent of WC hospital stays and 86 percent of estimated total allowances for inpatient hospital services. The five-year decline in acute-care stays between 2003 and 2008 (21.2 percent) is not unexpected because the number of injuries involving days lost from work declined nearly 29 percent over the same period.[5] Arguably, given the fewer injuries with time lost from work, the implementation of the MTUS guidelines (see Chapter Four), and the movement of services from inpatient to outpatient settings, one might have expected a greater decline. The total estimated OMFS allowances for acute-care hospital services decreased 4.8 percent from 2003 to 2005 and then increased 10.7 percent from 2005 to 2008, resulting in an overall 5.3-percent increase for the period. The relatively low rate of growth in total payments is attributable not only to the reduction in the number of discharges but also to the elimination of the prereform OMFS exemption for high-cost services (e.g., burns, trauma cases, tracheostomies).

Table 3.4
Number of Workers' Compensation Discharges and Estimated Payments for Stays in General Acute-Care Hospitals, 2003–2008

	2003	2004	2005	2006	2007	2008	5-Year Change (%)
Discharges	28,151	26,978	25,673	24,513	23,697	22,179	−21.2
Estimated payments ($ thousands)	409,224	394,268	389,387	405,470	417,973	430,946	5.3
Estimated payment per discharge ($)	14,537	14,614	15,167	16,541	17,638	19,430	33.7
Case-mix index	1.619	1.731	1.724	1.794	1.852	1.967	21.5
Average standardized allowance per discharge ($)	8,979	8,443	8,798	9,220	9,524	9,878	10.0

---

[5]   According to the Division of Labor Statistics, the total number of nonfatal occupational injuries and illnesses involving days lost from work were 223,500 (2003); 201,400 (2004); 179,400 (2005); 171,000 (2006); 168,200 (2007); and 158,900 (2008) (California Department of Industrial Relations, 2011).

On a per-discharge basis, estimated payments increased 33.7 percent. We decomposed the increase into two components: (1) the increase in the relative costliness of individual cases that is measured by the change in the case-mix index and (2) inflation and other changes in the composite rates that are measured by the increase in the average standardized allowance per discharge:

1. The case-mix index is a measure of whether there are changes in the average costliness of inpatient stays.[6] It is calculated as the average relative weight for the DRGs to which patients are assigned based on their diagnoses and procedures. The increase in the case-mix index between 2003 and 2004 largely represents the switch from the OMFS relative weights (which had not been updated since 2001) to the current Medicare relative weights.[7]

2. The average standardized allowance is determined by dividing the estimated allowance per discharge by the average case-mix index. There was a 5.9-percent decrease in the average standardized allowance between 2003 and 2004, which is attributable to the elimination of the OMFS exemption for certain high-cost types of cases. Since 2004, when this exemption was eliminated, the average standardized allowance has equaled the average composite rate for acute-care hospital stays and increases each year for inflation, as well as other changes in factors affecting the composite rate, such as the wage index. The increase attributable to inflation and other rate changes was 10 percent for the period.

Adequacy of Official Medical Fee Schedule Allowances

One measure of the adequacy of the OMFS allowances is to compare the allowances with the estimated costs of WC stays. Overall, we found that estimated OMFS allowances were, on average, 3 percent higher than costs before taking into consideration the additional pass-through payments for hardware used during complex spinal surgery.[8] However, there was substantial variation by type of stay. For some types of inpatient stays, the allowances are slightly less than estimated costs, whereas, for other inpatient stays, allowances are considerably higher than estimated costs. The underlying principle of DRG-based payment systems is that the allowance will exceed costs for some patients and will be less than costs for other patients but that, on average, the allowance will be sufficient to cover the costs of the inpatient stay and provide a reasonable rate of return. Generally, this principle applies to variation within a given type of stay (e.g., spinal surgeries) rather than variation across types of stays. Systematic underpayments for particular types of stays could create access problems for WC patients, while systematic overpayments could create incentives for unnecessary hospital admissions. Prior to the 2004 changes, the OMFS provided for DRG-specific adjustments for certain types of WC stays that were consistently more or less costly than they were for Medicare patients. We did not identify access or overutilization issues during our study that would indicate that the DRG-specific adjustments should be reinstituted; however, both the overall adequacy of the

---

[6] For purposes of computing the case-mix index for this table, we used the actual relative weights used for payment purposes except for 2003 exempt stays. We used the 2003 Medicare DRG relative weights for these stays in order to include them in the table.

[7] If the Medicare relative weights had applied in 2003, the case-mix index would have been 1.752.

[8] For comparison, the national private-payer payment-to-cost ratio is estimated at 1.27 in 2008 (MedPAC, 2010).

allowances and the appropriateness of the allowances for specific types of cases should be reexamined on a regular basis in the future.

Pass-Through for Spinal Hardware

Spinal surgery accounts for nearly 40 percent of allowances for acute-care inpatient hospital stays before considering the additional pass-through payments that are allowed for the costs (net of discounts and rebates) of spinal hardware and instrumentation used during spinal surgery. The pass-through payment is a deviation from standard Medicare rules that was originally established to ensure that WC patients have access to expensive hardware. Because a substantial portion (about 51 percent) of the Medicare rate used to determine the OMFS composite rate is for devices implanted during spinal surgery (Dalton, Freeman, and Bragg, 2008) and the 1.20 multiplier used to determine the OMFS allowance already provides a cushion for any higher costs the hospital might incur in caring for a WC patient, an issue is whether the additional payment is an unnecessary and duplicate allowance.

Aside from the duplicate-payment issue, there are at least three other concerns about the current pass-through system for spinal surgery. First, a pass-through payment for hardware costs provides no incentive for using the least costly medically appropriate alternative. Second, the policy imposes an administrative burden to both payers and hospitals. Hospitals must locate invoices and determine the applicable costs and associated discounts and rebates for each patient. Often, multiple invoices are involved for a single WC patient, adding to the administrative burden. Third, the policy creates the potential for abuse, especially because payers cannot easily verify that the invoiced items were used only for the WC patient and that the reported costs are net of discounts and rebates.

Adequacy of Payments for Spinal Surgery

We evaluated the adequacy of current payments for spinal surgery using three approaches. First, we compared the resources used by WC patients undergoing spinal surgery in 2008 with those for Medicare patients. This set of analyses compared device utilization, total charges, and length of stay, for WC and Medicare discharges in 2008. We found that, on average, WC patients used more types of devices than Medicare patients use but that fewer vertebrae were fused. However, using total charges as a measure of relative costliness, the WC patients had lower costs than comparable Medicare patients, despite the more-frequent use of spinal hardware for WC patients. Average charges per Medicare discharge were 6 percent higher than the average charges per WC discharge ($135,125 versus $126,491). WC patients also had a shorter average length of stay than Medicare patients. The adjusted Medicare average length of stay was 16 percent higher (4.4 days versus 3.8 days). Both the average charge analysis and

Table 3.5
Comparison of Amounts Implicit in 2009 Standard Official Medical Fee Schedule Allowances for Spinal Surgery, with Estimated Average 2009 Implant Costs

Type of Surgery	Estimated Average Implant Costs ($)[a]	Amount Implicit in the OMFS Standard Allowance ($)	Difference ($)
Noncervical spinal surgery	14,407	11,544	2,863
Cervical spinal surgery	5,960	5,350	610

[a] *Orthopedic News*, 2009.

the length-of-stay analysis indicate that WC patients are less costly on average than Medicare patients, before considering that the OMFS allowance incorporates an extra 20-percent margin beyond the Medicare rates.

In our second set of analyses, we measured the adequacy of the allowance by developing a ratio of estimated allowances to estimated costs for each type of spinal surgery. An allowance-to-cost ratio of 1.05 indicates, for example, that estimated allowances are 5 percent more than the estimated costs and are, on average, adequate to cover the costs. We estimated the ratios for all spinal surgeries in 2008 before consideration of the pass-through amounts and found considerable variation across the different types of spinal surgery. However, for the two most common types of spinal fusion, the estimated allowance-to-cost ratio was less than 1.0 (lumbar spinal fusion = 0.93, cervical spinal fusion = 0.95), indicating that some continued payment for spinal hardware is warranted (see discussion of options later in this chapter).

We conducted a third set of analyses that compared the amounts implicit in the standard OMFS allowance for spinal hardware (before the pass-through) with the estimated WC spinal-hardware costs. Because information on WC-specific device costs is not readily available, we assumed that average WC implant costs are similar to the average for all patients. Table 3.5 shows the results of the analysis for the two most common types of spinal surgery.

Potential Policy Options

The objectives in refining the policy for spinal-hardware pass-through payments are to (1) recognize that WC patients use more hardware than Medicare patients do, (2) eliminate the duplicate payment for hardware, (3) provide incentives for efficient use of resources, (4) provide financial protection for atypically high-cost cases, and (5) reduce administrative burden. There are two basic options for eliminating the duplicate payment:

- Create an add-on payment for the difference between the estimated average WC hardware costs and the amount implicit in the OMFS allowance (e.g., $610 for cervical fusions in Table 3.5). This option recognizes that WC patients have, on average, higher device costs than Medicare patients have. Relative to a pass-through payment, it reduces administrative burden and eliminates the incentives for unnecessary hardware usage. By basing the add-on on average hardware costs, the payment is not as accurate on a case-by-base basis. Consistent with the underlying DRG averaging principle, it assumes that hospitals have, on average, similar spinal-hardware costs, but it would disadvantage hospitals that systematically have above-average costs.
- Continue the pass-through but reduce the multiplier for the OMFS standard allowance to remove the amounts attributable to device costs. This approach increases payment accuracy by paying actual hardware costs on a case-by-case basis. However, it continues the incentives to provide unnecessary and costly hardware and continues the administrative burden of filing and processing bills for hardware.

These two policies are not necessarily mutually exclusive. For example, the first option could be implemented as a general policy but with hospitals being given an option of choosing the second option. However, any election should be made on an annual rather than case-by-case basis. A case-by-case election would consistently overpay the hospital for patients with lower-than-average hardware costs while paying actual costs for patients with higher-than-average hardware costs.

Inflationary Impact of Coding Improvement

In 2008, the Medicare program implemented MS-DRGs. The MS-DRGs improve payment accuracy by paying more for more–severely ill patients and less for other patients; however, the severity-adjusted rates have also led to unwarranted payment increases caused by improvement in coding and documentation. The increases are not attributable to real changes in patient severity but rather to improvement in the completeness with which complications and comorbidities are coded. Real changes in patient severity affect patient care costs; changes attributable to coding improvement do not affect patient care costs and should not lead to higher payments.

For Medicare patients, the Centers for Medicare and Medicaid Services (CMS) actuaries estimated that coding improvement in the first two years of the MS-DRGs increased the average case-mix index (and expenditures) by 5.4 percent (CMS, 2010a). The increase in the average case-mix index is built permanently into the MS-DRG relative weights during the annual recalibration process. Since these weights are used by the OMFS, the WC allowances are 5.4 percent higher because of Medicare coding improvement before considering any coding improvement that might have occurred for WC patients over the same period.

The Medicare law requires that the program eliminate the coding-improvement effect prospectively through the annual update factor for inflation. The adjustment is being made in installments so as to moderate the impact in any given year. Medicare's solution for removing the inflationary impact of coding improvement by reducing the update factor is not an administrative option for the WC program because the Labor Code specifies the annual update factor for WC composite rates. However, the AD of DWC has authority to adjust the OMFS allowances within the overall 120-percent-of-Medicare limit. This authority could be used to account for the effect of coding improvements by implementing either (1) a lower multiplier to the Medicare rate or (2) an adjustment factor to reduce the relative weights. Either approach would achieve the same result as a reduction in the inflation update factor to the composite rate. Removing the amounts built into the Medicare rates would result in a permanent 5.4-percent reduction in OMFS allowances for acute-care inpatient stays.

Official Medical Fee Schedule–Exempt Inpatient Hospital Services

The Labor Code specifies that specialty hospitals (e.g., rehabilitation hospitals and rehabilitation units of acute-care hospitals, psychiatric hospitals and psychiatric units of acute-care hospitals, and children's, cancer, and long-term care hospitals) should be paid on Medicare-based fee schedules effective January 1, 2005. There has been no regulatory action to extend the OMFS to these facilities. Currently, payment for inpatient services provided by these hospitals is based on rates the payer has negotiated with the hospital or, in the absence of negotiated rates, the amount on which the payer and hospital are able to agree for the individual case. In either case, the hospital's charges are likely to be a factor in determining payment. Hospitals have established charge structures that are significantly higher than costs. OSHPD 2009 financial data indicate that the average cost-to-charge ratio for specialty hospitals in California was 0.32. Thus, California's WC program is vulnerable to high hospital markups as long as these services remain exempt and, if a contract is not in place, to additional administrative costs for negotiating a payment amount.

We used the OSHPD data to investigate the magnitude of program vulnerabilities in continuing to exempt these facilities from the OMFS. In Table 3.6, we show the number of WC inpatient stays in the exempt hospitals in 2008 and summarize Medicare's fee-schedule

Table 3.6
Overview of Workers' Compensation Stays in Specialty Hospitals and Medicare Payment Methods

Type of Hospital	Number of Hospitals	Number of Discharges	Total Charges ($ millions)	Medicare Payment Method
Rehabilitation (including units)	65	859	50.9	Per-discharge rate based on impairment and functional status
Psychiatric (including units)	50	301	10.1	Per diem DRG-based rate
Long-term care hospital	10	98	8.8	Long-term care DRG–based rate
CAH	21	171	6.1	Cost
Cancer	2	29	2.8	Cost subject to a rate-of-increase limit
Substance abuse	10	49	1.1	n/a
All exempt hospitals and units		1,478	79.2	

NOTE: CAH = critical-access hospital.

methodology, which varies across the specialty hospitals.[9] In total, there were about 1,500 WC inpatient stays in specialty hospitals in 2008. Hospital charges for these stays totaled approximately $79 million. The OSHPD data do not include payment amounts, but we assume that only a percentage of the charges were paid. For example, for the rehabilitation hospital stays in the WCIS data, the reported payments were 65 percent of charges. WC patients were concentrated in rehabilitation and psychiatric facilities. Although there were only ten WC stays in long-term care hospitals, the charges for these stays totaled nearly $9 million. Medicare has special payment rates for stays in these three types of facilities that we discuss in greater detail in Appendix B. Medicare pays three other types of hospitals—children's, cancer, and critical access—using cost-based payment methodologies rather than predetermined rates. These hospitals also had relatively few WC stays.

For these low-volume specialty hospitals, it is probably not worth the administrative burden of implementing a Medicare-based fee schedule. Two feasible alternatives, both of which would require a Labor Code revision, would be to (1) continue to exempt these facilities from the OMFS or (2) pay a reasonable markup over the estimated cost for a given stay instead of adopting a Medicare-based fee schedule. The payment could be determined by applying a cost-to-charge ratio to the charges on the inpatient bill to estimate the cost and then multiplying by a factor, such as 1.2. Two potential sources for the cost-to-charge ratio are the Medicare program and the OSHPD financial data. Relative to a continued exemption, this method would provide a reasonable return with less administrative burden than negotiating a payment amount for individual cases.

---

[9] For consistency, records that do not include charges for the inpatient stay are not included.

Ambulatory Surgery Services Provided to Workers' Compensation Patients

In this section, we first provide summary of the major reform provisions affecting the use and costs of ambulatory surgery services, the most important of which was extension of the OMFS to ambulatory surgery facility fees. We then provide an overview of the trends in the use and cost of ambulatory surgical services from 2005 to 2007. Unlike the other categories of services, prereform data are not available on the use and cost of these services. We conclude by discussing two issues for which additional policy changes should be considered to improve the efficiency and quality of care: a reduction in the OMFS allowances for freestanding (nonhospital ASCs) and tightening of the rules pertaining to payment for ambulatory surgery facility fees.

Our analysis uses transaction-level data on ambulatory surgery facility services collected by OSHPD. The agency began to collect these data from all licensed providers furnishing ambulatory surgery beginning in 2005. We analyzed the OSHPD data for 2005–2007 only. The data for 2008 and later are affected by the Third District Court of Appeals *Capen v. Shewry* decision in September 2007 that clinics that are owned by a physician or group of physicians are excluded from licensure by the California Department of Public Health. Most physician-owned ASCs were licensed prior to the decision, and it is likely that most ambulatory surgery for which facility fees were payable are reflected in the data for 2005–2007. To the extent that some ambulatory surgery facilities are not represented in the data, the volume of services and expenditures are understated. The data for 2008 and later do not contain information on physician-owned ASCs and were not analyzed. A description of our methodology and more-detailed findings are in Appendix C.

Overview of Reform Provisions

Prior to 2004, facility services furnished in connection with ambulatory surgery and emergency services were exempt from the OMFS; payments for these services were based on rates the payer negotiated with the provider, which often led to unreasonably high payments. In the case of ambulatory surgery, the provider could be either a hospital or a freestanding ASC. SB 228 (2003) eliminated the exemption for these facility services effective January 1, 2004. As amended, Section 5307.1 of the Labor Code requires that the OMFS include allowances for ambulatory surgery.[10] Payment is limited in the aggregate to 120 percent of the amount payable under the Medicare program for comparable services furnished to hospital outpatients.

Medicare assigns hospital outpatient procedures to ambulatory payment classification (APC) groupings of clinically coherent procedures with similar costs. Each APC has a relative weight reflecting the costliness of the median procedure in the group relative to the median cost for a midlevel clinic visit. To determine payment, the relative weight is multiplied by a conversion factor. Additional payments are made for high-cost outlier cases. Under the OMFS, the maximum allowable fee is 1.2 times the Medicare payment rate. The same rates apply to ambulatory surgery performed in hospitals and in freestanding ASCs.

In addition to the expansion of the OMFS, SB 228 prohibited physicians from making referrals for outpatient surgery to clinics in which they have a financial interest unless they have (1) disclosed financial interest and (2) obtained preauthorization from a claim administrator.

---

[10] The OMFS was also expanded to hospital emergency facility services.

Trends in Ambulatory Surgical Procedure Volume and Payments

Between 2005 and 2007, the number of annual WC encounters for ambulatory surgery declined 8 percent, from 118,869 to 109,363 encounters. The decline is not unexpected because of fewer WC claims, which is offset to some extent by the long-term trend toward a shift of surgery from inpatient to outpatient settings. Despite the volume decline in WC encounters, total maximum allowable facility fees for ambulatory surgery increased 16 percent from $223.6 million to $258.7 million for the period.

- There were no major changes in the types and distribution of ambulatory surgical procedures. In 2007, nerve injections accounted for 30 percent of the procedures and 10 percent of the allowable fees. Arthroscopy procedures accounted for 29 percent of the procedures and 46 percent of the allowable fees.

- Table 3.7 shows the distribution of ambulatory surgery procedures across hospitals and ASCs. There was a slight increase in the proportion of surgical procedures performed in ASCs. In 2007, about 69 percent of ambulatory surgical procedures for WC patients were performed in ASCs, and 31 percent were performed in hospitals. Overall, the surgical procedures performed in hospital settings were more resource-intensive than those performed in ASCs (an average relative weight of 39.1 versus 34.7).

- The surgical procedures performed in an ambulatory facility setting are generally appropriate for that setting. With the exception of nerve procedures, relatively few procedures are performed on WC patients in the ambulatory surgery facilities that are commonly performed in physician offices (where a separate facility fee is not payable). Nerve injections that are commonly performed in office-based settings accounted for 2.5 percent of all WC nerve-injection procedures provided in a facility setting. Although payers might approve performing procedures in an ambulatory setting that normally require an inpatient setting, few of these procedures were performed as ambulatory surgery (0.4 percent of all ambulatory surgery procedures).

- For the same set of procedures, 31 percent of ambulatory surgery on WC patients was performed in hospitals, compared with 59 percent for other patients ages 18–64. Group health plans that contract with hospitals for a full range of services reduce the proportion of non-WC surgery that is provided in ASCs (Wynn, Hussey, and Ruder, forthcoming). Without these payer preferences and by paying the same amounts for services provided in hospitals and lower-cost ASC settings, the OMFS provides a financial incentive to furnish more care in ASCs.

Potential Changes in Ambulatory Surgery Center Payment Policies

Currently, the OMFS allows the same fees for surgical services provided in hospital and ASC settings. This policy was adopted in part because the Medicare list of covered ASC procedures and payment rates were outdated when the OMFS for ambulatory surgery fees was implemented (Wynn, 2004) and in part because of concerns over the adequacy of allowances based on the Medicare ASC fee schedule. Beginning in 2008, Medicare updated and revised its payment system (CMS, 2007). Medicare now pays for most ASC services under a system that parallels the payment system for hospital outpatient services but at a lower rate. For procedures that are commonly performed in a physician office, the ASC payment rate is capped at what would be payable for practice expenses if the procedure were provided in an office setting.

Table 3.7
Distribution of High-Volume Workers' Compensation Surgical Procedures, by Setting, 2005–2007

Type of Service	2005			Percentage of Services in Hospital, 2006	Percentage of Services in Hospital, 2007
	Total Number of WC Services	Percentage of Services in ASC	Percentage of Services in Hospital		
Nerve injections	61,197	75.2	24.8	24.1	21.4
Arthroscopy	48,303	64.7	35.3	35.7	31.3
Nerve procedures	14,371	66.2	33.8	31.6	32.6
Musculoskeletal procedures except hand and foot	13,466	64.8	35.2	34.8	30.8
Hand musculoskeletal procedures	8,882	60.8	39.2	38.4	35.4
Hernia/hydrocele procedures	5,604	50.7	49.3	59.5	57.1
Excision/biopsy	4,339	56.4	43.6	42.5	38.4
Skin repair	3,498	45.2	54.8	48.4	43.5
Treatment fracture/dislocation	3,384	52.0	48.0	47.6	43.9
Percutaneous implantation of neurostimulator electrodes, excluding cranial nerve	860	66.9	33.1	32.8	35.9
Laminotomies and laminectomies	751	63.1	36.9	40.2	32.7
Implantation of neurological device	430	60.7	39.3	36.9	39.4
Implantation of drug-infusion device	118	52.5	47.5	43.7	34.3
All surgical services	179,128	65.8	34.2	33.6	30.6

By linking payment levels to differences in the cost of providing services, Medicare policies reduce financial incentives to shift services from hospitals and physician offices to ASCs. Because ASCs have a lower cost structure than hospitals, focus on a narrower set of procedures, and take less time, on average, to perform a given procedure, the cost of providing ambulatory surgery in an ASC is less than in a hospital (Wynn, Hussey, and Ruder, forthcoming). The initial ASC rates were set at 67 percent of costs, which was consistent with findings from a separate study conducted by RAND researchers comparing the relative costliness of ASC and hospital outpatient surgery services in California.[11] However, ASC rates have declined in the annual rate-setting process and are 56 percent of the hospital rates in 2011.[12] Assuming that ASC costs continue to be about 67 percent of hospital costs, reducing the payment from 1.2 times the hospital payment rate for outpatient surgery to 1.2 times 0.67 percent of the rate should be sufficient to cover the cost of ambulatory surgery facility services and provide a reasonable rate of return without creating incentives to shift services to ASCs. This would result in a 0.80 multiplier to the hospital rate (0.67×1.2). Continuing to tie the OMFS rate for ASC services to the Medicare hospital rate has the advantage of ensuring a consistent relationship between the hospital and ASC rates over time and avoiding the administrative burden of establishing and maintaining a separate OMFS for ASC services (with different relative weights, geographic adjustment factors, and update factors).

A disadvantage of basing the OMFS for ASC services on a lower multiplier to the hospital outpatient rate instead of the Medicare ASC fee schedule is that it would continue to pay a facility fee for services commonly performed in an office setting. However, our analysis of the 2007 OSHPD data did not find a large number of office-based procedures being performed in an ASC, despite the current incentives to shift services from an office to an ASC. If services shift significantly in the future, this issue could be addressed at that time by implementing a limit specific to the allowances for those services.

The decision by the California Third District Court of Appeals in *Capen v. Shewry* has several other implications for the WC program. First, because physician-owned ASCs are no longer licensed by the state, the distinction has become blurred between an ASC that is entitled to receive a facility fee and a physician who performs a surgical procedure in an office and is not entitled to a separate facility fee. The OMFS rules allow facility fees to be paid to ASCs that are either Medicare certified or accredited by an accrediting agency approved by the Licensing Division of the Medical Board of California. Facilities might be accredited that do not meet Medicare certification standards or do not maintain the facility infrastructure and services warranting a separate facility payment.[13] Consideration should be given to revising the OMFS

---

[11] In a separate study funded by the U.S. Department of Health and Human Services, RAND researchers compared the relative costliness of ASC and hospital outpatient facility services using the OSHPD data (Wynn, Hussey, and Ruder, forthcoming). Their preliminary findings suggest that California ASCs' costs were 66–71 percent of estimated costs for hospital outpatient department surgeries in 2008, depending on whether professional contract expenses are included in the ASC cost measure. Multispecialty California ASCs had higher costs than single-specialty ASCs, but the differences were slight. In reporting their findings in a working paper, the authors caution that the results should be considered preliminary and exploratory. Their comparison was between the conversion factor used under the Medicare outpatient prospective payment system conversion factor and the average ASC expense per relative weight unit for all patients.

[12] The decline is attributable to differences in the hospital and ASC inflation factors that are applied to the fee-schedule conversion factors and adjustments to the relative weights that are made during the annual rate-setting process to ensure that aggregate ASC payments are not affected by changes in the APC logic.

[13] The medical board requires that any outpatient setting, ranging from a solo practice to a large, multispecialty ambulatory surgery setting where "procedures are performed using anesthesia, except local anesthesia or peripheral nerve blocks, or both . . . in doses that when administered, have the probability of placing a patient at risk for loss of the patient's life-preserving protective reflexes" be accredited or have Medicare certification (California Health and Safety Code Section 1248). To be Medicare certified, an ASC must be accredited by the Accreditation Association for Ambulatory Health Care (AAAHC), American Association for Accreditation of Ambulatory Surgery Facilities (AAAASF), the Joint Commission, or the American Osteopathic Association. These four organizations have standards that have been deemed to meet or exceed Medicare standards. However, they apply fewer standards to organizations that are not seeking Medicare certification. For example, ASCs seeking AAAHC accreditation for Medicare certification must meet the additional standards regarding patient rights, governance and credentialing, quality of care, and quality management and improvement that are not required of

rules to specify the level of accreditation required to receive a facility fee, e.g., a facility that has been deemed by an accrediting organization to meet Medicare standards.

A second implication of the *Capen v. Shewry* decision is that physician-owned ASCs are not required to submit either encounter-level data on ambulatory surgery patients or facility-level utilization or financial data to OSHPD. This limits the ability of the WC program to monitor the types of procedures that are being provided in an ambulatory setting and develop measures to assess the cost, quality, and access of services. The WCIS is not as useful for this purpose because it is not as complete and cannot be used to compare WC experience with other patient experience. Consideration should be given to revising the Business Code to require comparable reporting by physician-owned ASCs as other ASCs.

Outpatient Drugs and Other Pharmaceuticals

In this section, we discuss the fourth major component of payments for noninstitutional services: outpatient drugs and other pharmaceutical products. We first provide summary of the major reform provisions affecting the use and costs of outpatient drugs. We then provide an overview of the trends in the use and cost of outpatient drugs. We conclude with a discussion of potential policy changes that would improve control over the use and cost of drugs and other pharmaceutical products.

Overview of Reform Provisions

In response to rising costs for pharmaceuticals, several changes were made in the 2002–2004 time frame that affect outpatient drugs. These changes do the following:

- Require dispensing of a generic equivalent of a brand-name drug unless a physician specifically provides for the nongeneric drug or a generic is not available.
- Allow payers to establish pharmacy benefit networks to provide pharmaceuticals and medical supplies to WC patients. Implementing regulations have not been issued.
- Limit the maximum allowable fee for drugs under the WC system to the Medi-Cal fee-schedule amount.

Trends in Use of Outpatient Drugs

Despite the reform provisions affecting outpatient drugs, CWCI reports significant growth in both the average number of prescriptions and the average payment per claim for prescriptions (Swedlow, Ireland, and Gardner, 2009). One cause for the increase is physician-dispensed drugs. Initially, a loophole in the OMFS created a financial incentive for physician dispensing of repackaged drugs (manufacturer-produced drugs that have been repacked for in-office dispensing). When this loophole was closed in 2007, some physicians turned to dispensing

---

other ASCs and office-based surgery practices seeking only accreditation. AAAASF has separate accreditation levels for anesthesia, so that an office-based surgery practice could be accredited for Class A anesthesia (local only) and not have the capacity to provide the type of anesthesia services typically associated with ASCs. In addition to these four organizations, the Medical Board of California also recognizes accreditation by the Institute for Medical Quality, a nonprofit subsidiary of the California Medical Association. The institute uses standards developed by California physicians practicing in the ambulatory setting that are intended to meet the specific needs of California facilities but has not applied to have its standards deemed to meet Medicare requirements.

compound drugs and medical foods from their offices. CWCI reports that payments for compound drugs, convenience packaging of drugs and medical foods (co-packs), and medical foods grew from 2.3 percent to 12.0 percent of medication expenses between the first quarter of January 2006 and the first quarter of 2009 (Ireland and Swedlow, 2010).

Another important contributing factor has been a growing use of Schedule II medications (drugs with accepted medical use that have a high potential for abuse or addiction). According to CWCI, Schedule II drugs increased from 2 percent to 18 percent of all California WC prescription drug payments between 2005 and 2008 (Swedlow, Ireland, and Johnson, 2011). The CWCI findings cover a study period that predates the implementation of the MTUS guidelines for chronic pain, which address use of pharmaceuticals in pain management. The use of Schedule II medications subsequent to the implementation of the MTUS for chronic pain should be examined when the prerequisite data become available.

Potential Policy Changes

Compound drugs remain an area of potential abuse. The MTUS should be updated and expanded to address them as a product class. In addition to addressing the evidence base supporting the efficacy of ingredients frequently used in compounding, the guidelines should consider whether FDA-approved drugs should be tried prior to prescribing the compound drug. Similarly, the MTUS should address the medical appropriateness of medical foods.

Physician dispensing creates financial incentives that affect the use of compound drugs and other pharmaceutical products. California's pharmacy code of regulations includes within the definition of *pharmacy compounding* the preparation of drugs "for distribution of not more than a 72-hour supply to the prescriber's patients, as estimated by the prescriber" (California Code of Regulations § 1735.2). Our review of sample bills indicates that there might be issues with both the amount and the frequency of the drugs that are dispensed by some physicians. Recognizing that patient convenience is a reason for dispensing the initial supply, a reasonable approach would be to cover an initial physician-dispensed supply but not refills.

The pharmacy benefit network could be an effective tool in managing pharmaceutical benefits. However, implementing regulations are needed because many payers have been reluctant to enforce rules for a pharmacy benefit network without an approved network. Arguably, MPNs are the most important tool currently available to address growing expenditures for pharmaceuticals. As discussed in the next chapter, an employer has the right to establish MPNs and control care provided to injured workers throughout the course of the claim. Most payers have not used this tool effectively to ensure that appropriate care is furnished in a cost-effective manner. In our interviews, we identified several self-insured employers with more-selective contracting with physicians who agree to use pharmacies designated by their pharmacy benefit manager and to not dispense drugs to patients directly. These self-insured employers have not observed the types of issues reported in the CWCI analyses.

Summary of Potential Policy Changes

In this chapter, we have reviewed four major categories of medical services that have been affected by the reform provisions. Our review identified several opportunities to improve the value of care provided under the WC program by improving the incentives to efficiently furnish high-quality care. For physician services, implementation of a Medicare-based fee schedule would align payments with the resources required to provide care and improve the incentives to furnish medically appropriate care. The new fee schedule also provides an opportunity to align financial incentives with improved processes of care. The OMFS could be modified to include explicit fees for activities that are unique to work-related injuries. For example, Washington's quality-improvement initiative reimbursed physicians for calls to employers of injured workers to coordinate return to work and rewarded physicians who filed timely reports (Wickizer, Franklin, et al., 2004).

The relatively low overall payment levels for physician services have been an obstacle in implementing the resource-based fee schedule. To mitigate the redistributional effects of the fee schedule, increases in overall payment levels should be considered along with implementation of a resource-based fee schedule.

For hospital inpatient services, two policy changes that would eliminate unnecessary expenditures were identified: elimination of the duplicate payment for spinal hardware and removal of the inflationary impact of coding improvement from the OMFS allowances. With respect to ambulatory surgery facility services, establishing lower allowances for freestanding ASCs would increase the value of those services, reduce the financial incentive to shift care inappropriately from hospitals and physician offices, and generate program savings. Savings generated by reducing payments to these institutional providers could be used to increase payments to physicians and other practitioners. This would increase payment equity across types of providers without increasing total payments for medical treatment.

With respect to pharmaceuticals, it is too early to know whether the MTUS for chronic pain will address the issues identified with drug overuse. Additional MTUS guidelines are needed to address compound drugs and medical foods, and OMFS changes are needed to ensure that allowances are reasonable. However, California's WC experience with repackaged drugs suggests that "quick fixes" might address issues in the short term but that the issues are likely to reemerge in another fashion unless the underlying incentives are addressed. The benefits gained from making policy changes to ensure that compound drugs are medically appropriate and payments are reasonable are also likely to be temporary unless greater attention is given to improving the overall incentives. Relatively low OMFS allowances for E/M services are often cited as the impetus behind physician in-office dispensing. If a resource-based fee schedule is implemented that provides reasonable payments for E/M services, in-office dispensing could be curtailed either through revisions in the Labor Code or by payers including restrictions in their contracts with physicians. Ultimately, value for all services will be increased through selective contracting with high-quality, efficient providers and appropriately rewarding their performance.

CHAPTER FOUR

Medical Provider Networks

The MPN provisions were among the most–potentially significant provisions in SB 899. Under the provisions, a self-insured employer or insurer may establish an MPN to provide care to WC patients throughout their course of medical treatment. Unless a worker has predesignated a personal physician as his or her primary-care physician prior to his or her injury, the employer assigns the worker to a network physician for initial medical treatment. The worker is free to choose another provider within the network after the first visit but has very limited rights to receive out-of-network care. Some employers have continued to use an approved WC health care organization (HCO) in conjunction with an MPN, in which case the worker is required to receive care only from an employer-designated physician for the first 90 or 180 days, depending on whether the employer also provides group health coverage.

Employers and insurers seeking to establish an MPN submit an application to DWC that provides information on how the MPN will meet certain requirements stipulated in the Labor Code. The requirements include standards intended to ensure that workers have timely access to high-quality care and recourse to nonnetwork providers if medically necessary care is not provided within the network. HCOs are deemed to meet the standards. Once approved, MPN reapproval is required only if there is substantial modification in the MPN policies and operations.

Rising medical-treatment costs created the impetus for the MPN provisions. From the employer and insurer perspective, MPNs hold promise for reducing costs because they retain more control over the care that is provided and, through the MPN development process, can do more to ensure the quality of the providers that are treating injured workers. Potentially, quality can be improved through selective contracting, a requirement that providers follow the MTUS guidelines, and concentrating care with providers who have expertise in treating injured workers. From injured workers' perspective, MPNs represent some loss of provider choice, but they also hold the promise for improving access to care because they are an established network of available providers.

In this chapter, we focus on selected topics related to MPN operations that are key to understanding whether the MPN potential for improving the value of care provided to injured workers has been achieved. After providing an overview of the current MPN landscape, we explore MPNs' impact on access and the quality and cost of care. We had expected to examine these issues using the WCIS data; however, we were unable to do so because the indicator for MPN services was not reliably reported in the 2007 data and there is no identifier to associate services with specific MPNs. DWC recently clarified how MPN care should be reported in the WCIS so it might be possible to separate MPN care from other contract care in the future; however, a requirement to use a unique identifier for each MPN is still lacking. Given these data limitations, our findings draw heavily on interviews and four site visits to MPNs that we conducted early in the MPN implementation stage and the results from surveys conducted for DWC to examine access to care under the WC program. We conclude with a discussion of changes that would improve the administration of the MPN provisions.

Overview of the Medical Provider Network Landscape

The MPN provisions were effective January 1, 2005. In total, 1,625 MPNs have been approved as of March 2011, of which 786 were approved in the first six months and another 218 approved by the end of calendar year 2005. Since that time, 224 have either had their approvals revoked (primarily because of ineligibility to file as an MPN), withdrawn, or terminated (because, for example, the insurer applicant is no longer doing business in California). As of March 2011, there were 1,401 active MPNs (see Figure 4.1), the majority of which had insurers as the applicants for approval. The 471 self-insured MPNs include 30 MPNs formed by groups of self-insured employers.

Behind these numbers, there is a confusing array of interrelationships. Many insurance companies and some self-insured employers have applied for approval for more than one MPN; in total, 681 applicants submitted the applications for the 1,401 active MPNs. Of these, 521 have applied for a single MPN, while ACE American Insurance Company and Fidelity and Guaranty Insurance Company have 50 and 43 approved MPNs, respectively (see Table 4.1). Different third-party administrators and networks are involved when an insurer has multi-

Figure 4.1
Medical Provider Networks Active as of March 2011, by Type of Applicant

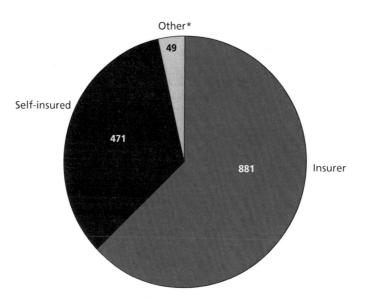

*Forty-seven of the applicants are California Joint Powers Authorities, and two are state entities.
SOURCE: California Department of Industrial Relations, undated (a).
RAND MG1144-4.1

ple MPNs. For example, among the 17 approved MPNs for Arch Insurance Group are the following:

- First Health CompAmerica Select MPN
- First Health CompAmerica Primary HCO Network
- ARCH/Gallagher Bassett/Coventry
- ARCH Coventry Network
- Gallagher Bassett Managed Care Services (GBMCS) MPN
- Sedgwick CMS MPN
- Sedgwick CMS Extended MPN
- Broadspire MPN
- Broadspire Signature Network
- MedInsights MPN accessing Prudent Buyer HCO.

The list includes MPNs formed from HCOs (e.g., First Health CompAmerica, Prudent Buyer). Other MPNs are identified with third-party administrators (e.g., Broadspire and Sedgwick CMS). Sedgwick CMS utilizes the Coventry MPN as its network but also offers an extended network that includes Kaiser physicians in addition to the Coventry physicians. The Coventry MPN is comprised of two wholly owned subsidiaries: the First Health and Focus networks. The HCO-approved First Health Primary is a narrow network that provides a "more tightly managed program in a more controlled access" program than the First Health Select (also HCO-approved) broad network that includes all physicians who have contracted with Coventry to provide WC services and meet its requirements (Coventry Workers' Comp Services, undated). The MPN approved for MedInsights, a division of Gallagher Bassett, uses Prudent Buyer HCO, a network operated by Anthem Blue Cross and Blue Shield. Untangling these relationships is challenging, and it is difficult to determine which entity assumes accountability for ensuring that the MPN standards are met. The applicant is responsible for meeting the standards but often relies on assurances from the organization managing the network.

As suggested by the list of MPNs approved for Arch Insurance Group, the actual number of physician networks that are in operation and the extent to which they have physician members in common is also difficult to determine. Because they are deemed to meet the MPN

Table 4.1
Distribution of Approved Applicants and Active Medical Provider Networks, by Number of Medical Provider Networks per Applicant

	Number of Applicants	Number of MPNs Applied For	Total Number of MPNs
	521	1	521
	133	2–5	346
	12	6–10	91
	13	11–20	190
	6	21–35	160
	2	36–50	93
Total	681		1,401

access standards and were exempted from filing a provider listing, HCOs were an attractive vehicle for quickly establishing an MPN. The majority of MPNs initially used HCO networks, but the proportion doing so has declined over time. An estimated 40 percent of active MPNs currently use HCO networks, with the largest being First Health Compamerica, Anthem Blue Cross Prudent Buyer, CorVel, and MEDEX Healthcare.

Once an MPN has been approved, reapproval is not required unless there has been a material modification in the MPN's policies or network composition. MPNs that were approved under emergency rules issued in December 2004 can continue to operate under those rules until they file for approval of a material modification, when they must also document how their policies conform to the final MPN regulations effective September 2005. As of June 2010, 808 applicants had filed 1,954 material modifications with DWC. Most material modifications have been required because the MPN rule defines a material modification as a change (increase or decrease) of 10 percent or more in the number or specialty of network providers since the approval date of the previous MPN plan application or modification. A common theme raised during our interviews with payers was the burdensome nature of this definition. DWC took steps to streamline the process effective October 2010. The new rules require that the applicant submit only the provider name, specialty, and practice location; by submitting the listing, the applicant is affirming that each physician listed has a valid and current license number to practice in California. Although the revised rules ease the administrative burden of filing the material modification, the definition is unchanged, and, perhaps more importantly, without licensure and tax identification numbers, it will be more difficult to examine such issues as provider network affiliations in a given geographic area.

The MPN penetration rate is uncertain, but it appears that most care is provided under an MPN contract or another contractual arrangement. Because the type of contractual arrangement affects policies regarding medical control, access and worker choice, and the appeal process for medical-necessity disputes, the pattern of care provided under an MPN contract might not be the same as the care provided under another contract. The distinction for data-reporting purposes might not always be clear cut because the MPN often uses an HCO network and some employers use the HCO network for initial care and, after the period of controlling provider choice within the HCO (90 or 180 days) has lapsed, switch to an MPN (which might use the same network of providers). The survey conducted by the University of Washington in 2008 found that, overall, 62 percent of responding providers reported currently contracting with an MPN.[1] The rate ranged from 42 percent for acupuncturists to 91 percent for occupational medicine physicians, but 18 percent of surveyed providers responded that they did not know whether they were in an MPN and are not included in the results (Wickizer, Sears, et al., 2009). CWCI's analyses on this topic are based on a sample of payers, each of which had networks in 2004 and MPNs in 2005–2008 and might not be representative of the overall WC system. Further, the CWCI analyses do not distinguish between MPN and other contract care. For its payer sample, the CWCI analyses document a steady increase in network care since 2004. The use of network providers across all first-year services provided after the first 30 days (the period during which the employer could control provider choice prior the MPNs)

---

[1]   The study population for the survey was licensed California providers eligible to function as primary treating physicians and who treated at least one injured worker within the WC system in 2004 or later. Ninety-two percent of the respondents reported that they were accepting or treating injured workers at the time of the survey, while 8 percent reported that they were no longer treating injured workers.

increased from 35 percent in accident year (AY) 2004 to 67 percent in AY 2008 (Ireland and Swedlow, 2010). For AY 2008, 61 percent of noninstitutional provider payments were made for contract care. Taken together with the University of Washington study, the CWCI analyses confirm that a significant and growing proportion of all services are being provided under MPNs.

We used the 2007 WCIS data in an effort to gauge MPN system-wide penetration rates. As noted earlier, the WCIS has an indicator that distinguishes between PPO (MPN care), other contract care, and care not provided under contract. The results show far lower-than-expected penetration rates for MPN care, suggesting that the indicator is not reliably used. The results are shown in Table 4.2. A combined MPN–other contract rate is most comparable to the CWCI statistic, although the WCIS statistics are for all accident years.

As seen in Table 4.3, the penetration rate is higher for newer injuries than for older injuries. The combined MPN–contract rate for AY 2007 is 59 percent, which is nearly the same as CWCI's finding with respect to the percentage of all first-year services paid for AY 2007 (60 percent). For AY 2004, CWCI found that 27 percent of payments for first-year services provided after 30 days from the date of injury were paid to network providers. The WCIS data show that 32 percent of 2007 payments for AY 2004 injuries made to noninstitutional providers were made to network providers, indicating that, although some care has moved to network providers, a significant portion remains outside-network care. The pattern is similar for payments for institutional care.

Table 4.2
Distribution of 2007 Medical Payments to Noninstitutional Providers, by Contract Status and Specialty (%)

Specialty	MPN Contracts	Other Contracts	Noncontract
Orthopedic surgery	23	34	43
Clinics	26	18	56
Physical therapy	21	42	37
Occupational medicine	18	52	30
Radiology	8	43	49
Physical medicine and rehab	9	62	28
Chiropractic	15	37	48
Other surgery	6	33	61
Anesthesiology	14	29	57
Internal medicine	14	36	51
Psychiatry	10	13	77

SOURCE: RAND analysis of 2007 WCIS data.

Table 4.3
Distribution 2007 Medical Payments to Noninstitutional
Providers, by Contract Status and Accident Year (%)

Year of Injury	MPN	Other Contract	Noncontract
2007	20	39	41
2006	13	34	53
2005	11	27	62
2004	9	23	68
2003	9	22	70
2002	7	21	71
Pre-2002	9	22	69

SOURCE: RAND analysis of 2007 WCIS data.

Access and Quality of Medical Care

The MPN provisions contain several standards intended to ensure that workers have adequate access to timely care. For example, the MPN must do the following:

- Employ a sufficient number of physicians to ensure that injured workers are provided treatment in a timely manner.
- Have a primary treating physician and emergency health care services located within 30 minutes or 15 miles of each workplace, and occupational health services and specialists located within 60 minutes or 30 miles of each workplace.
- Contract with at least three physicians of each specialty expected to treat common work-related injuries.
- Be capable of providing referrals to at least three physicians to an employee who lives or works outside the MPN service area.

The MPN provisions also contain standards intended to ensure that workers receive appropriate medical care. For example, the MPN must do the following:

- Contract with providers who agree to provide services consistent with the MTUS.
- Contract with occupational medicine specialists but also ensure that at least 25 percent of its contracted physicians treat primarily nonoccupational injuries.
- Have a plan that ensures continuity of care to workers for up to 12 months if a provider leaves the network.
- Have a plan to accommodate coordination of care for employees who suffered work-related injuries prior to the establishment of the MPN.

Meeting these standards and improving worker access to timely care requires networks that are made up of providers who are aware that they are in the network, are accepting new patients, and are knowledgeable about treating injured workers and the requirements of the California WC program (e.g., MTUS guidelines, documentation and filing requirements). DWC capacity to evaluate whether the MPN standards are being met is limited for several reasons. Insurers are not required to report the number of employers nor to identify which employers are covered under the MPN. The permanent regulations require that the applicant estimate the number of covered lives for the MPN, but those with multiple MPNs might not be reporting the covered lives specific to the MPN. Moreover, employer affiliations with MPNs are not static but change, for example, as they change insurers. Finally, as noted earlier, providers may be affiliated with multiple networks so that the provider-access standards for different MPNs can be met with the same group of providers. There might not be sufficient providers to handle the full WC caseload in the area. DWC has generally relied on two approaches to monitor compliance. First, the agency monitors and resolves complaints about MPN performance issues. Relatively few complaints—235—had been received as of May 2011. Second, the agency sponsored two surveys of WC patients and providers that examined access and quality issues related to WC medical care.

Survey Findings

Patient satisfaction is generally lower when patient choice is restricted through network requirements (Victor, 2003), but this is not always the case. A study of Pennsylvania injured workers who had access to panel physicians found better access to care and higher satisfaction with medical care among these workers (Pennsylvania Department of Labor, 2005). As shown in Figure 4.2, about the same percentage of California injured workers were satisfied with their care in 2008 as in the prereform period.

With respect to providers, Wickizer, Sears, et al. (2009) found that only 45 percent of providers agree that California's injured workers have adequate access to care. The survey respondents cited the following as the top five barriers interfering with care:

Figure 4.2
Trend in California Workers' Compensation Patient Satisfaction with Medical Care

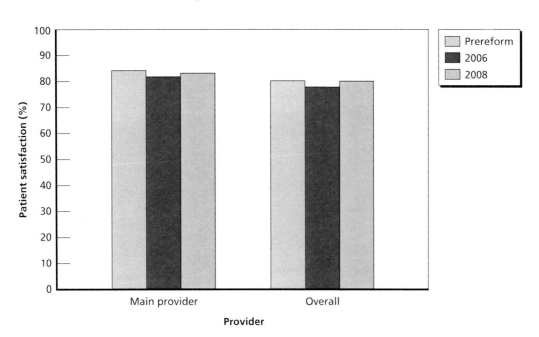

SOURCES: Victor, Barth, and Liu, 2003; Kominski et al., 2007; Wickizer, Sears, et al., 2009.
RAND *MG1144-4.2*

- delay in treatment due to UR
- denial of treatment due to UR
- administrative burden or paperwork related to UR
- ACOEM or MTUS guidelines too restrictive
- administrative burden or paperwork reporting requirements.

Moreover, one-third of the responding physicians intended to decrease their WC patient load or stop treating them altogether. Self-reported intention to make practice changes might not reflect real future reductions in physician practices; however, it might be a proxy for dissatisfaction with the system (Rittenhouse et al., 2004). Assessing the characteristics of the responding physicians, Wickizer, Sears, et al. (2009) identified the top barriers contributing to the probability that a physician intended to decrease or quit treating WC patients. The top barriers are

- unfamiliarity with WC laws or guidelines
- legal involvement
- administrative burden or paperwork
- inadequate or discounted fee schedule
- difficult claim adjusters or insurers.

Among the top barriers to access to care or contributing to the probability that a physician will treat WC patients, only the fee discounting is directly attributable to participation in an MPN (see the next section for a discussion of this topic). However, the other barriers are indicative of the failure of most MPNs (and there are notable exceptions) to meet their potential for improving the value of care provided to WC patients. From our interviews, we learned that the shortcomings are largely attributable to how the networks were formed. To quickly develop MPNs, many payers leased established networks without ensuring that the networks' members were aware of becoming MPN service providers and that they were willing to provide services to WC patients in accordance with the MTUS and accept, where applicable, discounted fees. Some networks have pruned out providers who are unwilling to take WC patients, but it is telling that 18 percent of the survey respondents in the 2008 survey did not know whether they were part of an MPN. In theory, the MPN physicians agree to provide services in accordance with the MTUS, but insufficient educational efforts are made to ensure that they are aware of the WC rules and MTUS, and most payers have not implemented targeted UR processes that would reward those network providers who do follow the MTUS. A potential benefit to physicians of network participation was increased WC patient load, which could offset some of the disadvantages of having OMFS fees discounted. However, higher patient workloads are less likely to materialize in a broad network in which patients have provider choice after the first visit. The shortcomings lead to frictional costs (those for medical-necessity and payment disputes) and provider dissatisfaction.

Use of Hospital Emergency Departments

Hospital ED services include not only care for injuries and other emergent conditions that require immediate treatment in EDs but also urgent care that could have been provided in a physician's office and nonemergent care that does not require immediate attention. A survey conducted for CHCF found several drivers for overuse of ED services: lack of timely access to routine medical care, generally poor communication between primary-care physicians and their patients, lack of awareness of alternatives to ED care, and positive attitudes toward quality and convenience of ED services, such as easier access to specialists and diagnostic testing (CHCF, 2006a). The survey results suggest that a finding of excessive use of ED services for nonemergent WC care would be an indicator of potential access problems and poor communication between patients and primary-care physicians.

In 2005, OSHPD began to collect transaction-level data on ED services (OSHPD, 2010). Because the OSHPD data are available beginning only in 2005, we cannot directly compare prereform ED usage with postreform usage. However, benchmarking data available from WCRI show only slight changes in ED utilization rates over the period for claims involving more than seven days of lost time valued on average at 12 months. Moreover, fewer claims used ED services in California than the median for the comparison group.

We investigated ED usage using the OSHPD encounter-level data for 2005–2007. Our methods and detailed findings are found in Appendix D. Key findings from our analysis of ED encounters for WC patients from 2005 to 2007 include the following:

- Most ED encounters for WC patients are for treatment of injuries. The proportion of ED encounters reported as initial treatment of injuries increased from 62 to 68 percent of total ED encounters during the study period.
- The volume of encounters that were for other than initial treatment of injuries declined 27.2 percent, compared to a 5.9-percent reduction in encounters for initial treatment of injuries.
- Statewide, about 20 percent of total WC encounters were either nonemergent or were emergent conditions that could have been handled in an office setting. There are county-level differences in these potentially inappropriate ED usage rates, but both urban and rural counties are among those with atypically high rates of potentially inappropriate ED usage.

The underlying question for our analysis was whether there is evidence of excessive use of ED services that might be indicative of potential access or quality-of-care issues following implementation of the reform provisions affecting WC medical care. We did not find indications that the recent reforms contribute to excessive use of ED services. Further, the disproportionately higher reduction in noninjury encounters is a potential sign of improvement in access to office-based care.

Payments for Medical Care

Care provided under an MPN should be more efficient than noncontract care. Although the MTUS applies equally to MPN and noncontract care, the MPNs have more potential for concentrating care with physicians with occupational health experience and coordinating care between the primary treating physician and specialists, thereby avoiding unnecessary services, such as duplicate imaging. In particular, a selective network is more likely to have established referral and communication patterns, and individual physicians are likely to treat more injured workers and be familiar with their special needs.

During visits to four MPN sites, we identified best practices that would further reduce the costs of MPN care relative to those for noncontract care. These included selective contracting with efficient providers, contract stipulations affecting service use (such as a ban on physician in-office dispensing of drugs), and provider education on the MTUS guidelines.

Selective contracting and provider education are important vehicles for eliminating unnecessary medical expenditures. The Labor code allows economic profiling to support these activities but expressly prohibits physician compensation from being structured to encourage reducing, delaying, or denying medical treatment or restricting access to medical treatment. The MPN provisions define economic profiling as any evaluation based on the economic costs or utilization of services associated with medical care provided or authorized by a physician, group practice, or independent practice association (e.g., a PPO network). The filing for MPN approval must include a description of the MPN's overall profiling methodology and how profiling is used in UR and peer review, as well as a description of any penalties or rewards used in the program and any retention or termination procedures. Our review of economic profiling policies submitted with selected MPN filings found that they are not detailed enough to indicate how economic profiling is currently being applied operationally and warrant closer examination.[2] According to our interviews when the MPN provisions were first implemented, a variety of criteria had been used to select network providers, such as word of mouth about the providers' quality; the physicians' reputation for providing thorough assessments, having good communication skills, and filing reports in a timely manner; limited economic profiling data; and willingness to accept discounted fees. Over time, as insurers have obtained more data on the services provided and ordered by network physicians, we would expect that there has been an increased use of economic profiling to inform provider educational efforts and target UR.

Contract stipulations can also be an effective way to improve the quality and efficiency of care. The potential benefits of this approach with regard to pharmaceuticals have been demonstrated by a large self-insured employer. This employer's contracts with network physicians require that prescriptions be ordered through network pharmacies and preclude physician in-office dispensing of drugs. In interviews we conducted looking at the compound-drug issue, we found that, unlike other payers, this employer was not experiencing problems with compound-drug usage (see Chapter Two for a discussion of this issue).

The general OMFS provisions apply to payment rates for network providers; namely, the OMFS allowance is applicable unless the payer and provider have agreed to an alternative amount. Fee discounting is the prevailing practice. A provider may agree to fee discounting in expectation of higher WC patient volume, particularly in a narrow network. However, the provider does not make an explicit decision to accept a lower fee for WC patients in leased network situations. Instead, the existing contractual arrangement between the entity managing the leased network and the provider governs the fee-discounting arrangement. We found in our interviews that this was a major source of irritation for physicians, who found that they had no choice about accepting WC discounted fees if they wanted to stay in the network for patients of other payers. Because the leased networks tend to be broad, the benefit of higher patient vol-

---

[2]   Studies by other RAND researchers have used medical bills for Massachusetts non-Medicare services to examine the different technical decisions necessary for creating cost profiles and the utility of cost profiles in selecting "more-efficient" doctors. The researchers found that common profiling methods result in 22 percent of physicians being assigned to the wrong cost category in a two-tier system (Adams et al., 2010). The methodological issues, such as attribution and definitions of the episode of care, might be somewhat different for WC medical services because there is a primary treating physician and the status of the WC claim could define the episode. Other issues, such as sample size and reliability, would be applicable.

umes in return for the fee discounting is unlikely to materialize. The 2008 survey conducted by the University of Washington found that 59 percent of responding providers reporting receiving discounted fees. Thirty percent reported receiving 1–15 percent off the fee schedule, and 29 percent reported a discount greater than 15 percent. Fifteen percent reported receiving payments at the fee-schedule level or higher, and another 25 percent were unable to report the applicable discount rate (Wickizer, Sears, et al., 2009). Among the survey respondents who were no longer treating WC patients, 21 percent ranked a payment-related factor (inadequate fee schedule, discounting, or payment denials) as the most important reason for no longer treating injured workers (Wickizer, Sears, et al., 2009). A concern expressed by some during our interviews is that the high-performing physicians who have other sources for patients will no longer treat WC patients, lowering the average quality of care received by WC patients.

Improving Oversight and Aligning Incentives for Value

Under the current MPN certification process, only the insurer or self-insured employer may apply for MPN approval. With a few notable exceptions, another administrative entity actually forms the network and contracts directly with network physicians. The payer contracts with that administrative entity to "lease" the provider network and does not directly contract with the physicians. The administrative entity leases the same network to multiple payers, resulting in different payers applying for MPN approval for the same group of providers. This creates unnecessary administrative burden and makes it difficult to assess the performance of individual MPNs. As a practical matter, accountability for network performance is not clearly established, and information needed to assess adequacy of network coverage is not obtained. Reapproval is required when there is a material modification (including a 10-percent change in network providers), but there is no recertification process, and the AD has no intermediate sanctions to impose for poor performance. Termination is the only recourse against MPNs that fail to meet the required standards. Several actions would reduce administrative burden and increase DWC's ability to exercise oversight:

- Revise the definition of *applicant* to mean the group of providers or entity that establishes the MPN (employer, insurer, or other administrative entity). This would streamline the approval process and better align legal accountability with operational accountability for meeting MPN standards.
- Require recertification every two to three years. This could be a streamlined process requiring only submission of any policy changes since last approval. It could be an across-the-board policy, or it could be triggered by poor performance on administrative measures or patient-satisfaction measures.
- Require an insurer to report annually on the name and federal employer identification number of employers using the MPN and the geographic service area for the employer (which could be smaller than the MPN service area). Currently, DWC has no information on whether particular employers are using the MPN and cannot assess MPN performance.
- Require the MPN to annually delineate service area and report providers by specialty, state licensure number, practice location, and geographic units within service area. Together with the annual reporting by employers, this would give DWC the capability to assess

the adequacy of network coverage and overlap of physicians participating in multiple networks. This would replace the requirement for filing a notice of material modification for changes in the size and composition of the network.

- Revise the WCIS reporting requirements to require a unique identifier for each MPN.
- Give DWC authority to impose intermediate sanctions (e.g., suspend new contracts with insurers or employers or impose monetary fines) rather than only revoke approval for failure to comply with MPN processes.

Currently, most MPNs are broad panels selected primarily to meet access requirements and provide fee-discounting opportunities. The Labor Code does not require that an MPN have credentialing or quality-assurance activities. The employer or insurer has the exclusive right to determine the members of its network but is not explicitly relieved of the burden of proving that due process was used in the provider-selection process. When provider networks are leased, a provider might not be aware of its responsibilities as an MPN provider. Most workers either are not aware of the right to predesignate or do not anticipate that they will have an injury that they would like to have treated by their personal physician. Potential changes to address these issues include the following actions:

- Require that the MPN have a credentialing and quality-assurance process and report annually on related activities. This could include any provider sanctions, summary of grievances or complaints and their resolution, provider educational opportunities, and patient access and satisfaction measures.
- Require that there be a written agreement between the applicant and the provider specifying (1) that the provider will treat WC patients, (2) that the provider will not charge the worker for services, (3) that the provider will abide by the MPN referral rules and the medical-treatment guidelines, and (4) the agreed-upon fees for services.
- Strengthen the Labor Code provision that allows the applicant to be selective in provider contracting. The Texas code, for example, specifies that provider exclusivity in contracting is not a restraint of trade violation.
- Allow an injured worker to designate his or her personal physician as primary treating physician after an injury occurs if (1) the worker received care from the physician within two years prior to the date of the injury and (2) the physician agrees to abide by the MPN rules and refer only to the MPN.

Although these are important steps to ensure a high-functioning MPN, the first two actions listed above could be left to the discretion of the MPN instead of being adopted as an MPN regulatory requirement. This would put the onus on employers to contract more selectively with MPNs that perform these functions and would avoid creating unnecessary burden for payers that already undertake similar activities. Other actions to improve value are generally within the purview of the MPN and would not be appropriate for regulatory action. Best practices used by some MPNs that payers should consider to increase value include the following:

- Use patient surveys to monitor timeliness and satisfaction with care, particularly with regard to specialty referrals, and whether the physician evidenced occupational health best practices, such as discussing return to work, and whether work restrictions are needed and how to avoid recurrent injury (as applicable).

- Ensure that patients have ready access to a current list of network providers that highlights those willing to accept new WC patients. This issue was particularly problematic in the MPN start-up period. Although it might have become less of an issue in the interim, facilitating a match between workers looking for care and specialists willing to take WC patients would increase timeliness of care and increase workloads for providers who are willing to treat WC patients.
- Reward high-performing physicians. These rewards can be monetary (e.g., higher payment rates) or nonmonetary (e.g., less UR) and need not depend on quality outcome measures (Wynn and Sorbero, 2008).

CHAPTER FIVE

Medical Cost-Containment Expenses and Activities

In this chapter, we first present data on trends in medical cost-containment expenses and an overview of adjustments that occur during the bill-processing process to determine final payment for a service billed by a noninstitutional provider. We then focus on two key medical cost-containment activities related to medical-necessity determinations—namely, UR and the appeal process—that have been affected by the reform provisions. For each, we provide an overview of the relevant reform provisions, summarize available information on how the processes are conducted, and discuss changes that should be considered to improve program oversight and efficiency.

Medical Cost-Containment Activities and Expenses

Medical cost containment refers to a set of practices used to monitor and manage the price, use, and volume of medical services and products based on clinical efficacy and need (Swedlow and Ireland, 2008). Insurers and self-insured employers use a wide range of techniques to manage medical costs, including case management and disease-management programs, UR, fraud detection, and selective contracting with medical providers.

Medical cost-containment expenses have been the fastest-growing component of WC medical expenses. According to CWCI, paid medical cost-containment expenses per indemnity claim valued at 12 months maturity have increased from $412 for AY 2002 to $1,511 for AY 2009, a 267-percent increase for the period (Figure 5.1). California had one of the highest average medical cost-containment expense levels among states routinely benchmarked by WCRI in both the prereform and postreform periods (Yang, Coomer, Radeva, et al., 2011).

Because the categories of medical cost-containment expenses are not reported separately, it is difficult to understand the reasons for the growth in medical cost-containment expenses and compare California's experience with that of other states. Because the number of WC medical bills has declined, medical bill-review costs, the major prereform component of medical cost-containment expenses that are typically paid on a per-bill or per–line item basis, should not be a major contributing factor to the growth. It is more likely that UR processes that review medical services for consistency with the MTUS and MPN leasing costs (which are either a flat fee or a percentage of savings) are the major contributors to growth of medical cost-containment expenses. Without reporting by the detailed cost categories, it is not possible to assess whether these activities are cost-effective. In particular, there is concern that the growth in medical cost-containment costs is attributable to payments for network leasing expenses attributable to fee discounting rather than expenses for case management or other programs

Figure 5.1
Trends in Paid Medical Cost-Containment Expenses per Indemnity Claim Valued at 12 Months, Accident Years 2002–2009

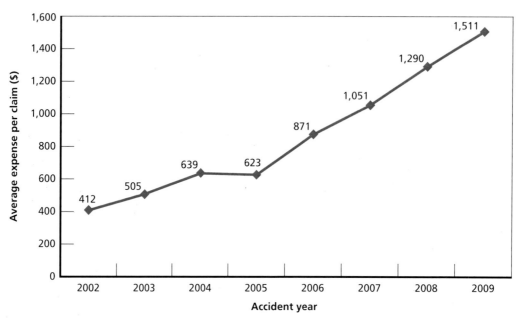

SOURCE: Ireland and Swedlow, 2010.
RAND *MG1144-5.1*

that might directly improve patient outcomes. As discussed in Chapter Four, the extent is unclear to which these leasing expenses are being used for selective contracting on the basis of quality and efficiency as opposed to simply to gain access to provider network organizations that are able to negotiate discounts with their providers.

Effective in 2010, an amendment submitted by the WCIRB was approved by the California Department of Insurance to reclassify medical cost-containment expenses from "medical incurred losses" to "allocated or unallocated loss adjustment expenses" (WCIRB, 2009).[1] This amendment also called for the clarification of the definition of *medical cost containment* within the *California Workers' Compensation Uniform Statistical Reporting Plan—1995* (WCIRB, 2011) and asked that medical cost-containment expenses as a category be reported separately from other costs so that they could be monitored (WCIRB, 2011). However, the list of cost-containment expenses defined in the amendment was not exhaustive, and there have already been indications that insurers have reclassified expenses so they can be counted as "medical benefits." Further disaggregation of medical cost-containment expenses into those that are directly related to medical care, such as care coordination and case management, and those

---

[1] The amendment states,

> The cost of [medical cost-containment] programs that cannot be allocated to a particular claim shall be considered unallocated loss adjustment expenses. These costs include, but are not limited to: (a) Bill auditing expenses for any medical services rendered, such as hospital bills, nursing home bills, physician bills, chiropractic bills, medical equipment charges, pharmacy charges, physical therapy bills and medical vendor bills. (b) Hospital and other treatment utilization reviews, including precertification/preadmission, and concurrent or retrospective reviews. (c) Access fees and other expenses incurred with respect to the utilization of managed care organizations (MCOs), such as PPOs, MPNs, and HCOs. (d) Costs of medical management except for nurse case management or case management that directly interacts and is coordinated with the injured employee and others, who are all parties to the employee's need for medical care.

that are related to administering the WC program, such as UR, legal fees, and network leasing, would facilitate monitoring these costs.[2] The recommendations of the National Association of Insurance Commissioners regarding the calculation of medical loss ratios (MLRs) for insurers (to comply with the provisions of the Affordable Care Act) under health care reform could be used as a model for the categorization.

Overview of Adjustments to Bills Submitted for Noninstitutional Services

We used the 2007 WCIS data to examine the types of adjustments that are being made on bills submitted by noninstitutional providers. The purpose of the analysis was to gain insights into the frequency and dollar value of different types of adjustments that are being made on submitted bills and how they differ between insurers and self-insured employers and between network and nonnetwork care. The analysis examines the disposition of bills that are submitted for payment and does not account for services that were denied prospectively and not furnished.

We divided the line items on the bills into two categories: those for which no payments were made and those for which some payment was made. Results are reported separately for self-insured plans and insured plans, and, within each, we report the value of adjustments separately for providers who are participating in a network and those who are not. For the line items for which no payments were made, duplicate billings accounted for the highest percentage of denials (Table 5.1). Duplicate billings are symptomatic of inefficiencies in the system and add to administrative burden. They reflect provider rebillings when a payment determination has been delayed and when there is provider dissatisfaction with the initial payment determination.

Fee reductions resulting from both application of the OMFS and additional discounting accounted for nearly one-third of the denied charges for network care and about one-fifth of the denied charges for nonnetwork care. Some of these denials are for separate billings for services that are included in a payment covering a package of services. About the same percentage of billed charges for contract and noncontract care was denied based on network rules. Examples of the types of reasons for denials in this category include services that were not authorized by the designated network or primary-care provider, those for which plan procedures were not followed in providing the service, or those for which the provider was not certified or eligible to be paid for the service (e.g., the services were provided outside the provider enrollment period, or an ambulatory surgery facility fee was billed by a nonaccredited entity). Other denials were related to medical-necessity determinations and are examined in a later section on UR.

For the line items for which some payment was made, the vast majority of adjustments are for fee-schedule adjustments (Table 5.2). Overall, 37 percent of billed charges were reduced for fee-schedule reasons, although this amount differed by insurer status and network status. As expected because of fee discounting, network providers paid by insurer plans had a higher percentage of billed charges reduced for fee schedules than nonnetwork providers did (37 percent versus 32 percent). For self-insured employers, however, network providers had a lower percentage of fee-schedule reductions in billed charges than noncontract providers did (43 percent

---

[2] The American Academy of Actuaries speculates that classifying all cost containment activities as administrative expenses might have the effect of deemphasizing the importance of cost-containment programs and could cause some insurers to stop using them, leading to higher premiums (Bell, 2010). Separate reporting by expense category would address this concern.

Table 5.1
Basis of Adjustment on Line Items with Zero Payment as a Percentage of Total Billed Charges, by Category, Insurer Status, and Contract Status (%)

Reason for Denial	Insured		Self-Insured Employer		Total		
	Network Care	No Network Care	Network Care	No Network Care	Network Care	No Network Care	All Bills
Duplicate billing	31	36	28	35	30	36	35
Billing error	3	3	3	3	3	3	3
Documentation	13	10	7	6	12	10	10
Medical necessity	4	10	4	4	4	10	8
Prior authorization	6	7	4	4	5	6	6
Fee reductions	29	14	49	42	35	21	24
Network provider rule	3	2	2	1	2	2	2

SOURCE: RAND analysis of WCIS data.

NOTE: The denominator for each cell is the total billed charges for all line items with zero payment for each combination of insurer and contract status. We defined the categories based on bill-adjustment reason codes. Network care includes MPN and other contract care.

Table 5.2
Adjustments on Paid Line Items as a Percentage of Total Billed Charges, by Category, Insurer Status, and Network Status (%)

Adjustment Reason	Insurer		Self-Insured	
	Network Care	Nonnetwork Care	Network Care	Nonnetwork Care
Fee schedule	37.1	32.0	43.2	46.6
Billing error	0.7	1.3	0.6	0.8
Documentation error	1.9	4.0	1.3	2.2
General coverage exclusion	0.2	1.5	0.1	0.4
Medical necessity	2.4	6.0	1.1	1.6
Prior authorization	1.1	2.8	0.6	1.0
Network rule	0.4	0.8	0.1	0.2
Not WC-related care	1.2	3.0	0.2	0.9
Other	0.5	1.0	0.7	1.1
Total	45.5	52.5	47.9	54.8

SOURCE: RAND analysis of WCIS data.

NOTE: The denominator for each cell is the total billed charges for all paid line items for each combination of insurer and contract status. We defined the categories based on bill-adjustment reason codes. Network care includes MPN and other contract care.

versus 47 percent). There are several limitations to interpreting the data on fee-schedule reductions. Billed charges are generally much higher than the amount that the provider actually expects to be paid under the OMFS, so a substantial difference between the billed charges and paid amounts is expected.[3] We were unable to distinguish reliably between reductions attributable to the application of the OMFS and additional reductions attributable to fee discounting; the reported reductions in billed charges are the combined difference between billed charges and paid amounts attributed to fee-schedule adjustments and contractual arrangements. The reported paid amounts represent what the insurer or self-insured employer paid for the service rather than the amount the provider received for the service. Under network arrangements, for example, a payer may pay 90 percent of the OMFS allowance; the entity managing the network may retain 5 percent of the allowance as a leasing fee and pay 85 percent to the provider.

Overall, providers participating in networks had lower total reductions in total billed charges than providers who do not have a contract (45.5 percent versus 52.5 percent for insured plans; 47.9 percent versus 54.8 percent for self-insured plans).

Figure 5.2 shows the distribution of billed charges for the non–fee-schedule adjustments on the paid bills. The majority of the adjustments are related to documentation issues and medical-necessity issues. These are discussed in the section that follows.

Figure 5.2
Distribution of Billed Charges for Non–Fee-Schedule Adjustments on Paid Bills, by Category, Insurer Status, and Network Status

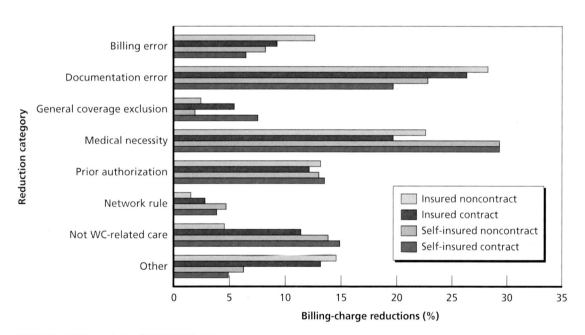

SOURCE: RAND analysis of WCIS 2007 data.
NOTE: The denominator for each bar is the total billed charges for all paid line items for each combination of insurer and contract status. We defined the categories based on bill-adjustment reason codes. *Network care* includes MPN and other contract care.
RAND *MG1144-5.2*

---

[3] For comparison, a study commissioned by the American Medical Association that examined the pricing policies for one large commercial insurer found that fee-schedule adjustments accounted for a 54-percent reduction in billed charges (American Medical Association, 2005).

Medical-Necessity Determinations

Both our stakeholder interviews and the 2008 University of Washington survey found that it was common for stakeholders to express concern over aspects of the medical-necessity determination process. In this section, we explore two key components of the medical-necessity determination process: UR and the dispute-resolution process for medical-necessity determinations.

Our ability to look at the issues of concern is limited. The bottom-line question (what is the quality of medical-necessity decisionmaking?) requires medical record review and cannot be examined using administrative data. A proxy measure, the percentage of UR denials that are overturned during the dispute-resolution process, is of limited utility because a high percentage of services are denied prospectively and might never enter the bill-processing system or appeal process. With these limitations in mind, we undertook several analyses:

- We summarized the findings from the UR investigations conducted by DWC. These findings do not address the quality of the decisionmaking process but do inform whether UR procedural requirements are being followed and provide an overview of the types of URs and decisions.
- We used the WCIS to explore the percentage of billed charges that are adjusted for medical necessity–related reasons initially and whether they are subsequently paid. The reversal of the initial denial could occur for a variety of reasons (e.g., the bill was initially processed incorrectly, the provider submitted additional documentation, the initial decision was reversed upon informal or formal review). We cannot tell the reason from the WCIS data.
- We used findings from the stakeholder interviews and interviews with regulators for other health programs, as well as regulatory information, to investigate alternative models for resolving medical-necessity disputes.

Utilization Review

UR provides formal oversight of the treatment that physicians provide to injured workers and can be used prospectively, concurrently, or retrospectively to review care to determine whether it is medically necessary.

Effective January 1, 2004, new UR processes required that a claim administrator file documentation with DWC either explaining his or her UR plan or identifying the external UR organization with which he or she has contracted to perform this function. The UR plan must be developed by practicing physicians, evaluated annually, disclosed to the treating physician and injured worker, and made available to the public. Regulations surrounding the enforcement of administrative penalties for failing to meet the procedures and time frames of UR required by the Labor Code were effective as of June 7, 2007. These regulations provide for routine investigations of UR practices of claim administrators and UR organizations every five and three years, respectively, and targeted investigations on an as-needed basis.

Provider Perceptions of Utilization-Review Processes

In our 2006–2007 stakeholder interviews, providers raised considerable concern over the UR process. Major concerns included

- the application of the MTUS (ACOEM) guidelines as "hard and fast" rules, with reluctance to approve any deviations from the guidelines
- across-the-board review of all services
- excessive and unreasonable levels of documentation being required to substantiate medical necessity
- delays in obtaining necessary care while UR was being conducted and initial determinations reviewed
- use of out-of-state UR physicians with unknown qualifications
- UR physicians who are pressured to meet productivity standards and process cases quickly rather than invest the additional effort to make a fully informed and appropriate coverage decision.

Our interviews were conducted after the UR regulations were issued but prior to the 2007 effective date of the enforcement rules for the UR processes; however, there is evidence that these provider concerns continued after the UR enforcement rules were adopted. As discussed in Chapter Three, the results from the 2008 survey conducted by Wickizer, Sears, et al. (2009) found that at least four of the top five physician-cited barriers to care were related to the UR process and strict application of the MTUS guidelines. Sufficient concerns remained about how to provide timely responses to physician requests for medical-treatment authorization and to ensure that workers receive medically necessary treatment that DWC convened a stakeholder meeting in 2010 to discuss potential changes to the UR regulations. DWC plans to address concerns raised at that meeting about what constitutes a valid request for treatment authorization by developing a standard request form through the rulemaking process (California Department of Industrial Relations, undated [a]). There are also two potentially encouraging signs. First, DWC has assigned a passing score to all but three UR investigations since the investigations were initiated in 2007. Second, there has been a decline in the number of expedited hearings on medical-necessity issues.[4]

Summary of Utilization-Review Investigation Results

DWC posts on its website the results of its investigations of UR practices. Because a random sample of cases is selected for investigation, the results provide an overview of UR activities (Table 5.3). Since 2007, DWC has conducted a total of 197 investigations involving 175 claim administrators, 22 UR organizations, and 13,800 cases. Nearly all requests for authorization (94 percent) are made prospectively—that is, UR is conducted prior to the delivery of requested services provided in other-than-inpatient stays. Concurrent reviews, which are conducted during hospital stays, constitute less than 1 percent of UR cases. Retrospective reviews, which are conducted after medical services are provided, occur in less than 6 percent of reviews. Across all cases that were investigated, 70 percent were approved, while modifications or delays for additional information occurred for 6 and 2 percent of the decisions, respectively. On average, 22 percent of review decisions were denials; the percentage denied by UR organizations was higher (25 percent) than for claim administrators (20 percent).

---

[4] It is not clear how much reliance should be placed on the decline. Expedited hearings rose from 10,321 in 2002 to a high of 14,642 in 2005 before starting to decline. In 2009, there were 8,614 hearings. In addition to fewer WC claims, changes were made in the reporting system in 2009 that might affect comparability with prior years.

Table 5.3
Summary of Requests for Authorization and Types of Utilization-Review Decisions for Cases Selected for Utilization-Review Investigations

Investigator	Year	Number of Investigations	Number of Cases Investigated	Type of Request for Authorization			Type of Decision			
				Prospective	Concurrent	Retrospective	Approve	Modify	Delay	Deny
Claim administrator										
	2007	7	372	356	0	16	292	22	11	48
	2008	67	2,404	2,220	2	182	1,720	151	42	488
	2009	47	1,806	1,702	5	99	1,181	99	44	479
	2010	49	1,843	1,770	9	64	1,295	106	33	397
	2011	5	2,215	2,126	9	80	1,587	128	44	445
	Total	175	4,430	4,252	18	160	3,174	256	88	890
							(70%)	(6%)	(2%)	(20%)
UR organization										
	2007	3	135	129	0	6	83	9	0	43
	2008	18	869	827	7	35	593	69	13	193
	2010	1	26	25	0	1	1	4	0	21
	Total	22	1,030	981	7	42	677	82	13	257
							(66%)	(8%)	(1%)	(25%)
Total		197	5,460	5,233	25	202	3,851	338	101	1,147
							(70%)	(6%)	(2%)	(22%)

SOURCE: California Department of Industrial Relations, undated [a].

The performance findings from the investigations are summarized in Table 5.4 separately for claim administrators (who may refer some cases to UR organizations) and UR organizations. The investigations focus on the UR procedural issues, and summary measures are reported for the timeliness of the responses, whether the content of the notice was proper, and whether the notice was distributed to the proper individuals. The notices must provide an explanation of the reasons for the claim administrator's decision, a description of the medical criteria or guidelines used to evaluate medical necessity, and the clinical reasons regarding medical necessity. The audit investigation reviews whether these elements are in the notice but does not evaluate the quality of the decisions. As seen in Table 5.4, most faulty responses involved timeliness of decisions. Overall, 7.5 percent of decisions involved an untimely response. The percentage of untimely responses for UR cases handled by claim administrators was lower (6 percent) than for UR organizations (13.9 percent). Most UR organization investigations were conducted in 2008 and might not reflect current performance. However, the discussion at the 2010 stakeholder meeting suggested that there are coordination challenges when a separate UR organization is used. Ten of the 18 UR organizations reviewed in 2008 were located out of state. The average performance rating for these organizations was similar to the rating for in-state organizations (data not shown).

DWC scores performance on sending the correct notices in a timely manner to the proper individuals. A passing score is a performance rating of 85 percent or higher. Across all investigations, the average performance rating was 95.5 percent. As noted earlier, only three investigations had performance ratings below 85 percent, two of which were for UR organizations surveyed in 2007. One UR organization received a passing score when resurveyed in 2010, while the other has been purchased by another medical bill-review organization. The claim administrator receiving a failing score was investigated in 2010 and has not been resurveyed. Each violation of a UR requirement has a monetary fine associated with it. The fines for more-serious violations are mandatory; they cannot be waived, but they can be mitigated at DWC's discretion based on the medical consequences and gravity of the violations, good-faith efforts to comply with the UR requirements, and the frequency of violations. The fines for minor technical violations may be waived if the performance rating is 85 percent or higher and may also be mitigated. In total, there have been 779 violations. The potential fines totaled $437,550, of which $160,425 were subject to assessment.

The UR investigation results provide an overview of the types of requests for authorization and the disposition of the requests but do not provide information regarding the types of services that are denied and whether initial denials are subsequently paid. We used the 2007 WCIS data to gain some insights into these issues. The analysis should be considered exploratory because of our limited ability to examine the issues. As noted above, most services are reviewed through a prospective review process, and those that are denied would not be captured in this analysis unless the services were nevertheless provided despite the adverse UR determination. Unfortunately, the WCIS data cannot be used to explore what happens after an adverse prospective review determination is received; instead, we are limited to analyzing the types of medical-necessity adjustments that are made during bill processing. Except in cases in which an adjustment is made for failure to obtain required preauthorization (which accounted for about 13 percent of the non–fee-schedule adjustments), we are unable to determine what type of UR applied to the service. To analyze the adjustments that were made for medical necessity–related reasons during bill processing, we extracted only bills that were initially paid before July 1, 2007, that reported an adjustment-reason code associated with

Table 5.4
Performance Results for Utilization-Review Investigations, 2007–2011

Investigator	Year	Number of Cases Investigated	Percentage of Requests with Faulty Responses			Average Performance Rating	Violations			
			Untimely Response	Faulty Notice Content	Improper Distribution of Notice		Number	Total Value of Fines ($)	$ Not Assessed	$ Assessed
Claim administrator										
	2007	372	9.9	0.5	2.4	95.5	50	4,750	4,750	0
	2008	2,404	9.6	2.5	1.9	86.6	379	263,800	121,400	142,400
	2009	1,806	7.4	0.1	1.6	96.8	188	112,350	58,700	53,700
	2010	1,843	6.2	2.6	0.4	97.2	192	64,550	11,950	52,600
	2011	2,215	5.2	1.0	0.0	96.4	242	69,300	16,700	52,600
	Total	4,430	6.0	1.6	0.4	97.0	484	138,600	33,400	105,200
UR organization										
	2007	135	24.4	20.0	9.6	80.3	80	4,100	300	3,800
	2008	869	12.1	6.9	1.0	93.5	204	294,250	242,825	51,425
	2010	26	19.3	19.2	0.0	87.2	11	600	600	0
	Total	1,030	13.9	8.9	2.1	91.4	295	298,950	243,725	55,225
Total		5,460	7.5	3.0	0.7	95.5	779	437,550	277,125	160,425

SOURCE: California Department of Industrial Relations, undated [a].

medical necessity. This allowed us to examine the outcomes of bill resubmissions over at least six months. Appendix A has a more detailed explanation of our methodology. Our results are summarized in Tables 5.5 and 5.6. Table 5.5 shows the proportion of billed charges that have a medical necessity–related adjustment (including a request for additional documentation) by type of service. The results are separately reported for insurer-paid bills and bills paid by self-insured employers. Across all services, 3.9 percent of the billed charges were denied for medical necessity–related reasons. A higher percentage of billed charges were adjusted for medical necessity–related reasons by insurers than by self-insured employers (4.7 percent versus 1.9 percent). Across all services, insurers adjust network care less often than nonnetwork care, but the pattern is not always consistent by type of service. It is likely that other reasons—such as the service being provided out of network—would have led to some denials of payment for nonnetwork care so that a medical necessity was not a reason for adjusting the bill. The lower rates for the self-insured bills could be indicative of better compliance with prior-authorization processes and decisions rather than differences in the retrospective UR process.

Using the same services that were reported in Table 5.5, Table 5.6 shows the percentage of billed charges that remained as medical necessity–related adjustments after at least six months, i.e., those that were not paid by the end of the calendar year. Overall, 2.5 percent of billed charges for which medical-necessity adjustments had been made remained unpaid (compared with the initial 3.9 percent). In other words, about 64 percent of the billed charges that had been initially adjusted for medical necessity–related reasons remained unpaid,[5] but the medical-necessity issues were resolved for about 36 percent of the billed charges. For the insurer-paid bills, the different patterns across type of services are revealing. About 20 percent $(1.0/5.1)$ of the network E/M services denied for a medical-necessity consideration within the first six months of 2007 remained unpaid by the end of the calendar year. This is in contrast to the chiropractic and physical medicine services provided by network providers, of which a substantially higher proportion remained unpaid. Overall, for insurer-paid bills, about two-thirds of the billed charges remained unpaid for services furnished by network providers, compared with nearly 80 percent for noncontract providers. Although relatively fewer self-insured employer bills were initially adjusted for medical necessity, a smaller percentage remained unpaid by the end of the calendar year.

Dispute-Resolution Process for Medical-Necessity Issues

Overview of the Postreform Process. The dispute-resolution process for WC medical-necessity issues is complex. It differs depending on whether the employer has established an MPN, whether the employee has predesignated a physician, and whether the injured worker is represented by an attorney. Within an MPN, one process applies if the injured worker and physician agree that medically necessary care has been denied through UR, and another process applies if the injured worker disagrees with the MPN physician about appropriate treatment. If the issue is not resolved during the initial dispute-resolution stages by an examination, as applicable, by a qualified medical evaluator (QME), an agreed medical evaluator (AME), or an independent medical reviewer (IMR), an injured worker with a compensable claim (or a claim under investigation) may request an expedited hearing on a medical-necessity issue by an administrative law judge at a DWC district office. An expedited hearing must be held within

---

[5] Sixty-four percent is $(2.5/3.9)$.

Table 5.5
Billed Charges Subject to Medical Necessity–Related Adjustments as a Percentage of Total Billed Charges, by Type of Service, Insurer Status, and Contract Status: Percentage of Total Billed Charges Initially Adjusted for Medical Necessity–Related Reasons

Type of Service	Insurer-Paid Bills			Self-Insured Employer Bills			
	Network Care	Nonnetwork Care	All Bills	Network Care	Nonnetwork Care	All Bills	All Bills
E&M	5.1	6.0	5.6	4.2	2.8	3.5	4.9
Chiropractic	3.6	9.9	7.8	2.1	3.8	3.2	6.5
Physical medicine	1.9	9.1	5.9	1.5	2.3	1.9	4.7
Major procedures, orthopedic	4.0	2.7	3.3	1.3	1.7	1.5	2.7
Major procedures, nonorthopedic	6.3	4.2	5.0	2.6	1.7	2.1	4.2
Minor procedures, musculoskeletal	4.4	3.6	3.9	1.8	1.6	1.7	3.3
Minor procedures, nonmusculoskeletal	4.2	7.8	6.5	1.5	2.6	2.1	5.4
Advanced imaging	1.1	5.1	3.7	0.2	1.0	0.6	2.8
Other imaging	1.6	7.3	5.1	0.6	1.4	1.0	3.9
Other services	2.2	4.5	3.7	1.2	1.3	1.3	3.0
All services	3.2	5.7	4.7	2.0	1.9	1.9	3.9

30 days of receipt of the declaration of readiness. (If the compensability determination has not been made, the regular hearing process applies, which requires that the hearing be held within 75 days.) Either party not agreeing with the judge's decision may file a request within 20 days for reconsideration by the Workers' Compensation Appeals Board (WCAB), a seven-member judicial body appointed by the governor and confirmed by the state senate. A party may apply to the court of appeals for review of a final decision of the WCAB (Labor Code § 5950), similarly to an appeal from a trial court decision in civil litigation. Compared with the volume of cases at the trial level and appellate level, relatively few cases are accepted for review at the appellate level, and the scope of appellate review is limited (Labor Code § 5952).

Streamlining the Appeal Process and Improving Quality of Decisions. In our 2006–2007 interviews, some stakeholders expressed concerns about the complexity, timeliness, and appropriateness of the dispute-resolution process for medical-necessity determinations. The current independent medical review (IMR) process for MPN medical-necessity disputes is not functional because workers may simply keep changing physicians when there is a dispute over appropriate medical care. The number of requests to DWC for QME panel lists has more than doubled since the reform provisions were implemented and has posed challenges in providing timely and appropriate QME reviews. Although the spike in QME requests appears to have been resolved by mid-2009, scheduling problems continue because of mismatches in the demand and supply of specific specialties. For example, orthopedic specialists account for only 25 percent of registered QMEs, but an orthopedic specialty is requested 45–65 percent of the time (CHSWC, 2010a). Further, a large share of expedited hearings and many regular hear-

Table 5.6
Billed Charges Subject to Medical Necessity–Related Adjustments as a Percentage of Total Billed Charges, by Type of Service, Insurer Status, and Contract Status: Percentage of Total Billed Charges Flagged for Medical-Necessity Review Not Paid Within at Least Six Months

Type of Service	Insurer-Paid Bills			Self-Insured Employer Bills			All Bills
	Network Care	Nonnetwork Care	All Bills	Network Care	Nonnetwork Care	All Bills	
E&M	1.0	4.1	2.5	0.5	0.8	0.7	1.9
Chiropractic	3.2	9.1	7.1	1.3	2.4	2.0	5.7
Physical medicine	1.4	8.2	5.2	0.9	1.8	1.3	4.0
Major procedures, orthopedic	0.7	1.4	1.1	0.4	0.4	0.4	0.9
Major procedures, nonorthopedic	1.8	3.0	2.5	1.2	1.4	1.3	2.2
Minor procedures, musculoskeletal	1.7	2.2	2.0	0.7	1.0	0.8	1.7
Minor procedures, nonmusculoskeletal	1.7	4.5	3.5	0.7	1.4	1.1	2.9
Advanced imaging	0.4	4.7	3.2	0.1	0.9	0.5	2.4
Other imaging	1.0	6.6	4.4	0.4	1.2	0.8	3.4
Other services	1.1	3.6	2.8	0.6	0.8	0.7	2.1
All services	1.1	4.5	3.2	0.6	1.0	0.8	2.5

ings involve medical-necessity issues. When medical-necessity issues reach hearings, judges make decisions based on their understanding of evidence presented to them, but the rulings on medical-necessity issues are not decided by medical experts in the medical treatment at issue.

Increasingly, health plans and insurers are resolving medical-necessity disputes through external review by an independent medical review organization (IMRO). Although the specifics of external review programs differ, a survey conducted for the Kaiser Family Foundation found that the programs generally share the following characteristics (Dallek and Pollitz, 2000):

- *Independence and fairness.* The review organization and reviewers are independent from both parties to the dispute, and consumers perceive the process as fair.
- *Clinical expertise.* The reviewers are clinical experts in the specialty field that commonly treats the medical condition at issue.
- *Efficiency.* Reviews take place within established time frames and are generally cost-effective.

Potentially, external review of medical-necessity issues could reduce the complexity of California's dispute-resolution process and increase the timeliness and appropriateness of medical-necessity appeal determinations. Typically, the first step in the dispute-resolution process is an internal reconsideration of the UR decision. An individual who is dissatisfied with the internal reconsideration decision may request review from an IMRO by a clinician who is knowledgeable with the treatment at issue. There are various models that use external review organizations in deciding medical-necessity disputes in the issues following an internal reconsideration of an adverse medical-necessity decision by the health plan or UR carrier. The following are some examples:

- Enrollees in California's commercial health care service plans and health insurance may request an IMR of an adverse medical-necessity decision.[6] A single IMRO processes all IMRs for both programs. An enrollee who does not agree to an IMR forfeits judicial appeal rights. Either party (enrollee or plan) may request judicial review of an IMR decision.
- The Texas WC program has an IMR process for medical-necessity issues that is separate from the dispute-resolution process for other medical-related WC issues, such as compensability and permanent disability determinations and fee-schedule disputes. Multiple IMROs (which are also used in the Texas commercial health plan dispute-resolution process) process the IMRs. A claimant or provider may request an IMR, and either party may appeal an IMR decision.
- The Medicare program uses similar IMR processes for medical-necessity issues arising under its fee-for-service and managed care plans. Under each type of coverage, a single IMRO processes the IMRs. Following an adverse IMR decision, the enrollee (but not the health plan) may request review by an administrative law judge. Either party may appeal the administrative law judge's decision to the Medicare Appeals Council and request judicial review of an adverse IMR decision.

A comparison of these three models and discussion of their implications for the WC program is in Appendix E. Following the general approach used by the Texas WC program, an IMR process could become the single route for appeals of adverse medical-necessity UR decisions while retaining the QME/AME process for other medical-related issues that require WC-specific expertise. This means that both the IMR process and the QME/AME process would apply for some claimants with multiple issues in dispute, but it is likely that the overall efficiency of the system would be improved:

- DWC would no longer need to issue QME panel lists for medical-necessity issues only or maintain a separate version of an IMR process for situations involving a dispute between a claimant and a medical network provider.
- The additional medical exams required before an IMR can be requested when the claimant and the medical network provider do not agree on medically necessary care would be eliminated.[7]
- Timely and impartial IMR decisions would minimize the need for expedited administrative hearings on issues of medical necessity.

---

[6] Similar IMR processes apply to medical-necessity issues arising under health plans and health insurance. California's Department of Managed Health Care oversees the health plans. The California Department of Insurance oversees the health insurance carriers. In addition to medical-necessity issues, the IMR process is used when the plan denies coverage because a treatment is experimental.

[7] Existing law requires the patient to obtain second and third opinions within an MPN before seeking an IMR to challenge the opinions of the MPN physicians (Labor Code §§ 4616.3 and 4616.4).

- The IMR process could provide for accelerated reviews for urgent cases using the current UR rules for an expedited review (i.e., there is a serious threat to the claimant's health or the normal time frame for a decision could harm the worker's ability to recover fully).

It is also likely that the IMR process will improve the appropriateness of medical-necessity determinations:

- The quality and documentation of UR reconsiderations would likely improve because payers would know that these decisions would be reviewed by individuals who are clinical experts in the medical treatment at issue.
- Most medical-necessity issues would be decided by medical experts instead of by judges in an administrative process.

To reinforce the use of the IMR process, a limit could be established on the number of times the worker may change physicians within the same specialty without MPN permission (e.g., several states provide that the employee may change initial provider twice and authorized specialist twice). This would encourage resolution of medical-necessity disputes through the dispute-resolution process rather than through switching providers and reduce inefficiencies inherent in changing physicians.

Improving Program Oversight and Administrative Efficiency

In this chapter, we have reviewed medical cost-containment expenses and selected medical cost-containment activities related to medical-necessity determinations. Medical cost-containment expenses have been the most rapidly growing component of WC medical expenditures, and the recent WCIRB decision to require separate reporting of medical cost-containment expenses is important because it will allow separate measurement of payments for medical care and medical cost-containment expenses. However, more-detailed reporting by category of expenses would allow a better understanding of the cost drivers and an assessment of the cost-effectiveness of different activities.

The medical-necessity decisionmaking process has been a subject of continuing concern. Program oversight could be improved by compiling and releasing additional information obtained during the UR investigations, i.e., information on the medical service for which medical review is sought and the nature of the decision. A high proportion of denied claims for a particular type of service could indicate deficiencies in the MTUS guidelines or need for additional provider educational activities. Similarly, a review of the medical services for which an expedited hearing is sought, as well as the outcome of the review, could inform whether changes are needed in the MTUS. Such efforts could be beneficial not only in improving medical decisionmaking at the provider and payer levels but also increase system efficiency by reducing duplicate billing and medical-necessity disputes. Last, consideration should be given to adopting an independent medical review process for resolving medical disputes. It would streamline the existing appeal processes and improve the quality of the medical-necessity decisions.

CHAPTER SIX

Monitoring System Performance

The purpose of this chapter is to provide an overview of the purpose of system performance measurement, describe a conceptual framework for monitoring system performance that could be used with a focus on medical care delivered to injured workers, and assess the potential for using the WCIS to monitor system performance.

This chapter consists of four sections. First, we describe the overall purpose of performance measurement. Next, we present a conceptual framework for the range of domains that could be addressed in a performance-measurement system and provide examples of measures that fall into each domain. This section builds on the groundwork laid in the RAND working paper *Medical Care Provided California's Injured Workers: An Overview of the Issues* (Wynn, Bergamo, et al., 2007). In the third section, we focus on performance measurement using low-back pain as an example. We used a literature review to identify potential measures and applied two measures that could be constructed with administrative data using the WCIS. In the last section, we summarize the limitations and challenges to using the WCIS to monitor system performance.

Performance-Measurement Overview

The overarching purpose of performance-measurement systems is to provide information that will enable policymakers and other stakeholders to identify areas in which performance is suboptimal. This then allows for the prioritization of identified issues, as well as the development of policies and interventions that will facilitate improvements in performance. These same systems then can be used to evaluate the effects of reforms and interventions.

Conceptual Framework

A comprehensive WC performance-measurement system would include measures that assess all aspects of WC. In Figure 6.1, we present a measurement framework for WC, adapted from Wynn, Bergamo, et al. (2007). There are three levels in this model: the provision of care, system costs, and system performance. We briefly describe each of these levels and the domains that fall within each level. Table 6.1 presents examples of measures that fall within each domain and that could be used in a performance-measurement system. The measures listed in Table 6.1 are included in either ongoing measurement activities or special studies conducted by parties involved in WC in California and other states. Table 6.1 is not meant

Figure 6.1
Workers' Compensation Performance-Measurement Framework

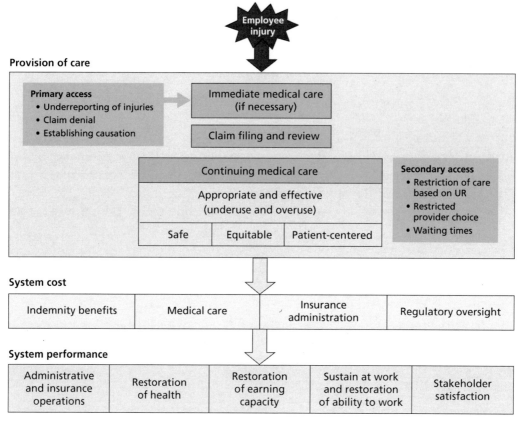

SOURCE: Adapted from Wynn, Bergamo, et al., 2007.
RAND MG1144-6.1

to be comprehensive, nor is it meant to imply that these measures can be developed from the administrative data in the WCIS.

Level one, provision of care, starts with the work-related injury of the employee; the incidence and type of injury vary by industry, safety provisions undertaken by the employer, and employee behavior. Access to care is a principal function of the system. There are two components to access: primary access, which is being able to enter the system and is a precursor to receiving care, and secondary access, which is being able to receive care after entering the system (Fox, Victor, and Liu, 2006). Primary access to medical care is influenced by underreporting of injuries, claim denial, and the effort involved in establishing causation. Secondary access is influenced by restrictions on medical care due to UR, restricted provider choice, and waiting times for appointments. An injured worker having access to care does not guarantee that the continuing medical care received is high-quality care. High-quality care is treatment that is appropriate and effective. This means striving to avoid both the overuse and underuse of services, as well as providing care that is safe, equitable, and patient-centered. These five characteristics plus efficiency are characteristics of a high-performing health system (Institute of Medicine [IOM], 2001). The second level captures system costs, which include the costs of indemnity benefits provided to injured workers, medical care costs related to the injury (which includes the IOM's efficiency domain), and the costs of insurance administration and regula-

Table 6.1
Example Measures for a Workers' Compensation Performance-Measurement System

Measure Category	Example of Measures
Provision of care	
Potential need for medical care	Number of nonfatal occupational injuries and illnesses; incidence of nonfatal occupational injuries; percentage of injured workers who did not work after reporting an incident
Immediate need for medical care	Percentage of injured workers seen by a doctor within 48 hours; average duration from date of injury to first nonemergency treatment
Claim filing and review	Timeliness of first report of injury or illness; number of claims filed
Continuing medical care	Ability to schedule a doctor's appointment (survey); ability to get needed care (survey)
System costs	
Indemnity benefit costs	Average indemnity cost per claim; average benefit payment per claim with more than 7 days of lost time
Medical care costs	Total charges for health care provider services; total paid amount for health care provider services; average medical payment per claim; percentage of medical payments by provider type (e.g., physician, chiropractor, hospital)
Insurance administration costs	Average medical cost-containment expenses; percentage of claims with medical cost-containment fees; average medical-legal expense per claim with medical-legal expenses
Regulatory oversight costs	Average benefit-delivery expense per claim with benefit-delivery expenses
System performance	
Administration and insurance operations	Time for injured worker to receive first WC benefit check; average number of days between MCO receiving FROI notice and date claim is electronically filed; percentage of injured workers who receive accurate benefits
Restoration of health	Mean medical recovery time
Restoration of earning capacity	Number of vocational rehabilitation awards issued; ratio of return-to-work wage to preinjury wage for vocational rehabilitation participants
Restoration of ability to work	Median time away from work; percentage of injured workers taking longer than 30 days to return to work; percentage of vocational rehabilitation cases with return to work
Stakeholder satisfaction	Customer satisfaction with hearing process; employer satisfaction; medical provider satisfaction; number of complaints received; satisfaction with medical care received; percentage reporting WC same as or better than other health care

NOTE: FROI = first report of injury.

tory oversight. The third level, system performance, is comprised of five domains: administrative and insurance operations, the restoration of the injured worker's health, restoration of the worker's earning capacity, sustaining the injured worker at work and restoration of his or her ability to work, and stakeholder satisfaction.

Performance Measurement

The measures selected for any performance-measurement system should be based explicitly on programmatic goals, such as improving clinical quality of care or reducing the growth in medical care spending. Numerous organizations have established criteria for the selection of clinical performance measures. These include that the measure

- be important—that is, that it addresses an area in which performance is known to be low or in which wide variation exists
- be methodologically sound and based on valid scientific evidence
- be feasible to implement—that is, that the data necessary to construct the measure either exists or can be collected without undue burden
- have an impact—that is, that the area the measure addresses creates a burden on the health of the population or the cost of care.

Measuring Quality of Care

The gold standard for the measurement of overuse and underuse is the medical chart. Although the use of medical-treatment billing records is attractive because they are readily available and capture services delivered to patients, there are potential limitations associated with their use, even assuming that the data are complete. There are concerns that administrative data created for the purpose of billing for rendered services lack the clinical specificity to adequately identify the necessary information to support quality-of-care measures, as well as risk-adjust outcome measures as necessary, and that the details of clinical care provided in the administrative data might not accurately reflect information in the patient's chart (Romano and Mark, 1994; Quan, Parsons, and Ghali, 2004; Fowles et al., 1995; Fowles, Fowler, and Craft, 1998; Horner et al., 1991; Romano, 1993; Solberg et al., 2006). Furthermore, performance measures supported by administrative data are narrower in scope than those supported by medical records. It has been shown that measured performance using administrative data appears higher than when performance is assessed with a broader set of measures using medical records (MacLean et al., 2006).

Although methodologically sound and evidence-based measures can be identified through a search of measure repositories and the literature, assessing potential measures against the other measure-selection criteria requires a level of understanding of the data that will be used for ongoing monitoring. If the criterion "feasible to implement" requires the use of measures that can be constructed using medical-treatment data, the measures will be more limited because few quality measures can be constructed using administrative billing data. Many more measures are available that can be constructed using chart review as the primary data source for performance measurement.

Measuring System Performance for Low-Back Pain

To evaluate the feasibility of using the WCIS for performance measurement, we focused on low-back pain. Low-back pain is a natural area of focus for WC performance measurement. In California's WC system, medical back problems without spinal-cord involvement were the second-most common claim diagnostic group (based on the Dyani Diagnosis Medical Grouper) in 2007 (Swedlow, Ireland, and Gardner, 2009). Admissions for back-related issues accounted for approximately 30 percent of total WC inpatient payments in 2005, and the DRG "Spinal Fusion Except Cervical" was the single DRG representing the greatest portion of payments (14.2 percent) (Appendix B).

We conducted a web search of National Committee for Quality Assurance (NCQA) Healthcare Effectiveness Data and Information Set measures, National Quality Forum—

approved measures, CMS imaging-efficiency measures, and measures included in the Agency for Healthcare Research and Quality National Quality Measures Clearinghouse to identify measures for low-back pain. Of the 20 measures that we identified (Table 6.2), only two

Table 6.2
Back-Pain Measures

Measure	Population	Measure Description	Source	Specs	Data Source
Underuse measures					
Initial assessment	Patients ages 18–79 with a diagnosis of back pain at the initial visit	Percentage of patients ages 18–79 with a diagnosis of back pain or undergoing back surgery who had back pain, function, patient history, prior treatment and response, and employment status assessed during the initial visit to the clinician for the episode of back pain	NCQA	Y	Medical recorda
Physical exam	Patients ages 18–79 with a diagnosis of back pain at the initial visit	Percentage of patients ages 18–79 with a diagnosis of back pain or undergoing back surgery who received a physical examination at the initial visit to the clinician for the episode of back pain	NCQA	Y	Medical recorda
Advice for normal activities	Patients ages 18–79 with a diagnosis of back pain at the initial visit	Percentage of patients ages 18–79 with a diagnosis of back pain or undergoing back surgery who received advice against bed rest lasting 4 days or longer at the initial visit to the clinician for the episode of back pain	NCQA	Y	Medical recorda
Advice against bed rest	Patients ages 18–79 with a diagnosis of back pain at the initial visit	Percentage of patients with medical-record documentation that a physician advised them against bed rest lasting 4 days or longer	NCQA	Y	Medical recorda
Mental health assessment	Patients ages 18–79 with a diagnosis of back pain with evidence of back surgery, epidural steroid injection, or more than 6 weeks of pain	Percentage of patients ages 18–79 with a diagnosis of back pain for whom documentation of a mental health assessment is present in the medical record prior to intervention or when pain lasts more than 6 weeks	NCQA	Y	Medical record
Recommendations for exercise	Patients ages 18–79 years with back pain lasting more than 12 weeks	Percentage of patients with back pain lasting more than 12 weeks with documentation of physician advice for supervised exercise	NCQA	Y	Medical record
Patient reassessment	Patients ages 18–79 with a diagnosis of back pain or undergoing back surgery	Percentage of patients with documentation that the physician conducted reassessment of both pain and functional status within 4–6 weeks of the initial visit or of a surgical procedure	NCQA	Y	Medical record

Table 6.2—Continued

Measure	Population	Measure Description	Source	Specs	Data Source
Shared decisionmaking	Patients ages 18–79 who had surgery	Percentage of patients with whom a physician or other clinician reviewed the range of treatment options, including alternatives to surgery, prior to surgery; to demonstrate shared decisionmaking, there must be documentation in the patient record of a discussion with the patient that includes treatment choices, risks and benefits, and evidence of effectiveness	NCQA	Y	Medical record
Assessment and management of chronic pain	All patients 16 years and older who meet the criteria for chronic pain (cervical and lumbar pain; headache; other disorders of soft tissues, myalgia/myositis and unspecified fibromyositis or related diagnosis) who are prescribed an opioid	Percentage of patients diagnosed with chronic pain who are prescribed an opioid who have an opioid agreement form and urine toxicology screen documented in the medical record	ICSI	N	Medical record/claims
Appropriate/overuse measures					
Appropriate imaging studies	Patients with back pain lasting 6 weeks or less	Percentage of patients ages 18–79 with a diagnosis of back pain for whom the physician ordered imaging studies during the 6 weeks after pain onset, in the absence of "red flags"	NCQA	Y	Medical record
Use of imaging studies	Patients ages 18–50 with a new episode of back pain	Percentage of patients with an ambulatory encounter for low-back pain who received an imaging study conducted on the episode start date or in the 28 days following the episode start date	NCQA	Y	Medical record/claims
Repeat imaging studies	Patients with more than one imaging study and patients with only one imaging study and no documentation in the medical record of physician asking about prior imaging	Percentage of patients ages 18–79 with a diagnosis of back pain who received inappropriate repeat imaging studies in the absence of red flags or progressive symptoms	NCQA	Y	Medical record

Table 6.2—Continued

Measure	Population	Measure Description	Source	Specs	Data Source
MRI lumbar spine	Patients with a diagnosis of low-back pain	Percentage of patients who had an MRI of the lumbar spine with a diagnosis of low-back pain for whom there are indications in the claim file of antecedent conservative therapy	CMS	Y	Claims
Imaging studies	Adults with low-back pain	Percentage of patients with a diagnosis of back pain for whom the physician ordered imaging studies during the six weeks after pain onset, in the absence of red flag	ICSI	N	Medical record/ claims
Appropriate use of epidural steroidal injections	Patients ages 18–79 years with a diagnosis of back pain or undergoing back surgery	Percentage of patients with back pain who have received an epidural steroidal injection in the absence of radicular pain and those patients with radicular pain who received an epidural steroid injection without image guidance	NCQA	Y	Medical record
Surgical timing	Patients ages 18–79 who have had back surgery	Percentage of patients without documentation of red flags who had surgery within the first 6 weeks of back-pain onset	NCQA	Y	Medical record
Outcome measures					
Lumbar functional status	All patients treated at outpatient rehabilitation clinic for whom both admission and discharge self-report "Lumbar Functional Status Measure" questionnaires were completed	Mean change score in lumbar functional status for patients with lumbar impairments receiving physical rehabilitation	Focus on Therapeutic Outcomes	N	Patient survey
Structural measures					
Patient education	Patients ages 18–79 with a diagnosis of back pain or undergoing back surgery	Educational materials provided to the patient that review the natural history of the disease and treatment options, the risks and benefits, and the evidence	NCQA	Y	Materials
Postsurgical outcomes	Patients ages 18–79 with a diagnosis of back pain or undergoing back surgery	A physician's system of examining postsurgical outcomes that includes (1) tracking specific complications of back surgery and periodic analysis of surgical-complication data and (2) a plan for improving outcomes	NCQA	Y	Electronic or paper report

Table 6.2—Continued

Measure	Population	Measure Description	Source	Specs	Data Source
Evaluation of patient experience		Evidence of (1) an ongoing system for obtaining feedback about patient experience with care and (2) a process for analyzing the data and a plan for improving patient experience	NCQA	Y	Patient survey instrument

NOTE: ICSI = Institute for Clinical Systems Improvement.

[a] Indicates measures collected for the Physician Quality Reporting Initiative (PQRI) using CPT II codes.

measures can be collected solely from administrative data. The source for the other measures included the medical report (12), administrative data supplemented by the medical record (two), patient survey (one), and physician reporting (three).

In addition to searching measure repositories, we also examined the literature for measures of medical care service use that have been utilized in research studies, which can be constructed using medical administrative data. These focused on the use of categories of services, such as primary care, specialty care, back-pain specialty care (orthopedics, neurology, neurology, neurosurgery, rheumatology, physiatry outpatient departments), physical therapy or occupational therapy, mental health services, computerized tomography (CT) and magnetic resonance imaging (MRI), spine X-rays, ED services, hospitalizations, and pharmaceuticals. These measures identify the percentage of patients receiving services within a specified period of the time of injury and average annual costs of services (Ritzwoller et al., 2006; Pham et al., 2009).

Utilization Measures

As stated previously, measure selection should focus on measures that (1) are important, (2) are methodologically sound and evidence based, (3) are feasible to implement, and (4) have an impact. Although methodologically sound and evidence-based measures can be identified through the approach described in the previous section—a search of measure repositories and the literature—assessing potential measures in view of the other measure-selection criteria requires a level of understanding of the data that will be used for ongoing monitoring. If the criterion "feasible to implement" requires the use of measures that can be constructed using medical-treatment data from the WCIS, the number identified through measure repositories (i.e., those supported by evidence) is reduced from 20 to just two, one that focuses on the use of MRI of the lumbar spine and one that looks at imaging more broadly within the first 28 days after a new injury. Performance on the two measures that can be constructed with medical bill data, as presented in Figure 6.2.

These measures can be supplemented with a broader array of utilization measures, the selection of which can be based on their potential impact. As the cost of WC continues to rise and California continues to be among the most expensive in the country, the inclusion of performance measures focusing on utilization and costs of services is natural. A first step to determining what type of utilization measures to include in a performance-measurement system involves understanding the the types of providers who receive payments for the treatment of low-back injuries and the types of services provided. Physician services represented 50 percent of total WC payments for individuals with back pain (data not shown). Nonphysician providers, such as chiropractors and physical therapists, accounted for 21 percent of payments, while other ambulatory clinics received 11 percent of payments. To further understand the types of utilization that contribute substantially to medical-treatment costs, we examined the types of services reported in the noninstitutional bills in the WCIS (Figure 6.3). Pharmacy comprised the largest share (24.3 percent); one of the identified measures that required medical-record review focused on pain assessment and management. Physician office visits comprised the next-largest share (17.1 percent); seven of the identified medical record–based measures focus on appropriate assessments and recommendations by physicians. Medical-legal evaluation and testimony represented the next-largest category of costs (11.4 percent). Physical medicine comprised 9.8 percent of payments, and back procedures 7.4 percent of payments. However, for some subsets of injured workers, surgery is quite common. Yang and colleagues reported that 38 percent of WC neuropathic back cases in fiscal year (FY) 2006 in California with more than seven days of lost time from work received surgery within 24 months of injury (Yang, Coomer, Landes, et al., 2010). In cases in which surgery occurred, it was a significant cost driver. The average total medical payment per episode was almost $21,000 with inpatient surgery but just over $7,000 with outpatient surgery (Yang, Coomer, Landes, et al., 2010).

One advantage of utilization measures is that they can frequently be applied to a broader patient population than appropriateness of care measures can. For example, Figure 6.4 shows that 12 percent of the people receiving medical treatments for low-back injuries in 2007 received an MRI or CT and slightly more than 30 percent received an X-ray. These measures include in the denominator all persons with lower-back injuries during the year. In contrast, only a subset of the individuals who received an MRI are included in the MRI appropriate antecedent-care measure in Figure 6.1. Of those who did receive an MRI, only 16.5 percent were eligible for the appropriateness measure, meaning that their injury occurred in 2007, they had one of the specific inclusion diagnoses, and they did not have any of the exclusion diagnoses. Utilization

Figure 6.2
Distribution of Payments, by Type of Service for Noninstitutional Bills for Lower-Back Injuries

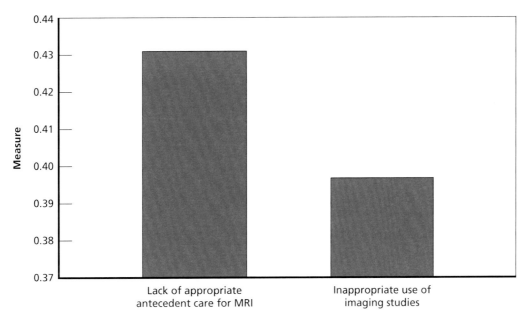

SOURCE: WCIS 2007, analysis of noninstitutional bills.
RAND MG1144-6.2

Figure 6.3
Back-Pain Imaging Utilization Measures

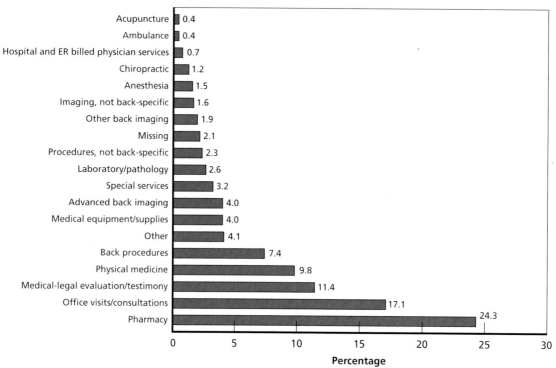

SOURCE: WCIS 2007, analysis of noninstitutional bills.
RAND *MG1144-6.3*

Figure 6.4
Back Pain Treatment Appropriateness Measures

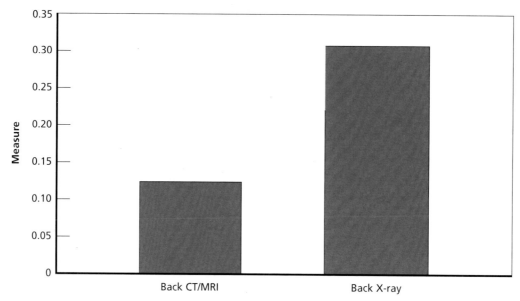

SOURCE: WCIS 2007, analysis of noninstitutional bills.
RAND *MG1144-6.4*

measures do have disadvantages, however. Case-mix adjustment might be necessary to ensure "apples-to-apples" comparisons.

Limitations and Challenges in Using the Workers' Compensation Information System to Monitor Performance

In this section, we discuss two challenges to using the WCIS for monitoring system performance more fully: lack of complete medical claim data and lack of measures that can be constructed with medical claim data.

Lack of Complete Data

Complete and reliable reporting to the WCIS is key to monitoring system performance. At present, due to incomplete data, a performance-monitoring system cannot rely solely on WCIS data even for those measures that can be constructed from administrative data. There are several ways in which the data could be incomplete: (1) a subset of employers and insurers do not report any data into the system; (2) employers and insurers report data for some but not all of the medical-treatment services provided to injured workers; (3) data that are submitted into the system are missing information for some data elements; or (4) data are reported inaccurately.

Medical data reporting is required for all services provided on or after September 22, 2006. DWC reports that WCIS data are incomplete, with approximately 11–12 percent of claims not reported into the system and only approximately 50 percent of FROI matched with medical-treatment data (California Department of Industrial Relations, 2011). This form of incomplete data will result in underestimates of total WC costs. However, as long as (1) the employers and insurers that report into the system do not differ substantially from nonreporting entities and (2) those entities that do report provide data on all medical treatments received by injured workers, estimates of cost per person, distributions of the types of services received, and percentage of injured workers receiving specific treatments produced using WCIS data should be valid and unbiased. The greater the differences between reporting and nonreporting entities in terms of the types of jobs performed, characteristics of the workforce, and types of behavior or providers delivering medical treatment, the more likely that estimates produced using WCIS data will not accurately represent the performance of the WC system at large. Until there is better compliance in data repoorting, it might be preferable to focus analyses on the "good" reporters—those trading partners that report data accurately and completely in a timely manner—but this effort also requires understanding whether their claims (in terms of patient and provider characteristics and of payer administrative processes) are representative of the WC system at large. For example, "good" reporters might also be more proficient at complying with other WC administrative requirements. Whether a subset or all of the reported data are used for performance monitoring, it will be important to examine and address the representativeness issues in analyses using the WCIS data.

Section 138.6 of the Labor Code, which sets out the AD's authority with respect to reporting requirements for the WCIS, does not include penalties for the failure of a claim administrator to comply with the electronic data–reporting requirements. Notably, two of the three other states with medical data-reporting requirements—Florida and Texas—both have financial penalties associated with failure to comply with reporting compliance. Texas has very high compliance standards; achieving such standards is probably possible only when requirements are paired with financial penalties for noncompliance. (Like California, Oregon does not have any penalties.)

Another form of incomplete data occurs when information needed for performance monitoring is not collected. California has adopted International Association of Industrial Accident Boards and Commissions (IAIABC) standards for medical data reporting. DWC does not have the authority under Section 138.6 of the Labor Code to require claim administrators to provide data elements that are not included in the IAIABC standards. For example, IAIABC standards do not require a unique identifier for services provided by an MPN that would facilitate analyses across MPNs. The IAIABC does have a process for enhancing data standards, which DWC has used to obtain standards for reporting lump-sum medical settlements, but the process is time-consuming and burdensome. Although DWC could use this approach as a method to enhance the data that are reported to the WCIS, giving DWC the authority to deviate from the IAIABC standards following a rule-making process would reduce the administrative burden associated with implementing needed changes in data elements.

Limited Use for Quality Measurement

Many more measures are available that can be constructed using chart review as the primary data source for performance measurement. However, the collection of these data would place a substantial time and financial burden on medical providers who would have to collect and report data. This burden might decline as more providers implement electronic medical records in accordance with provisions included in the federal Patient Protection and Affordable Care Act (Pub. L. 111-148, 2010). Until the use of electronic health records is widespread among providers in the WC system, measuring performance using medical claim administrative data is likely be the most feasible approach to performance measurement. Another alternative is to have providers report data on any measures that they report to other entities for other measurement programs, such as CMS's Physician Quality Reporting System. This system, however, requires providers to report on all payer data, not just WC patients. To the extent that the requirements and incentives that are part of the WC lead physicians to treat these patients differently than other patients, measures constructed using all-payer data might not reflect the care delivered to injured workers.

Summary

This chapter provided a brief discussion of performance-monitoring systems and a conceptual framework for the range of domains that could be addressed in a performance-measurement system. We then provided an overview of the measures that have been developed to assess the care delivered to individuals with back pain. There are many significant challenges to implementing a performance-monitoring system that focuses on medical care delivered to injured workers. To date, very few measures assessing the appropriateness of care for back pain can be supported using only medical claims. These, combined with measures of utilization selected with input from providers and other stakeholders, could form the initial efforts to measure performance. Combining these with appropriateness and utilization measures focusing on other common types of injuries would make the monitoring system more well rounded. These efforts could be enhanced and built on as new measures become available, as the use of electronic medical records becomes common, and as more information is reported through other measurement activities, such as the Physician Quality Reporting System. Even for those measures that can be constructed using administrative data, the feasibility of using the WCIS for this purpose is limited until DWC is provided with tools to enforce compliance and the flexibility to add needed data elements.

CHAPTER SEVEN

Increasing the Value of Workers' Compensation Medical Care

Recommendations

The medical-treatment system for WC is complex and multifaceted. We have limited our review to selected aspects of the system that were affected by the reform provisions and for which we believe further policy changes would improve system performance. Although this is the appropriate focus for this study, it is important that the improvements that the reform provisions brought to the WC medical system not be slighted. The changes were far-reaching and have important benefits. Consider, for example, the following:

- The principle of evidence-based medicine was introduced into the medical-necessity decisionmaking process by replacing the presumption favoring the primary treating physician with the MTUS.
- The UR provisions established a more open process with enforcement provisions for meeting established standards.
- Taken together, the caps on chiropractic and therapy visits, the MTUS, and the UR process addressed the provision of medically unnecessary services and brought service use in California's WC system more in line with other states.
- The MPN provisions laid a foundation for improving the quality and efficiency of care through selective contracting while protecting and potentially improving access to care.
- The expansion of the OMFS to ambulatory surgery facility fees and other services using Medicare-based fee schedules (and the Medi-Cal fee schedule for pharmaceuticals) reduced the level of contention in the system, as well as payment levels, while providing for a regular update process.
- Overall, the changes reduced annual medical expenditures and lowered the trend line for paid medical losses.

Nevertheless, average medical losses per indemnity claim at 12 months valuation were at their lowest level immediately after the implementation of the reform provisions in 2005. Since then, the expenses per indemnity claim have increased 13.1 percent annually—a considerably higher rate of growth than in group health (Figure 2.4 in Chapter Two). This higher rate of growth prompts concerns about whether further policy changes are needed to create better incentives for the efficient delivery of high-quality care under California's WC program. In our review of selected issues, we have identified additional policy changes that would improve the incentives for efficiently providing medically appropriate care, increase accountability for performance, facilitate monitoring and oversight, and reduce administrative burden.

Improve Incentives for Efficiently Providing Medically Appropriate Care

As discussed in Chapter Two, the value of medical treatment would be improved by doing the following:

- Implement a resource-based fee schedule that provides for regular updates and equitable payment levels.
- Create nonmonetary incentives for providing medically appropriate care in the MPN context through more-selective contracting with providers and reducing UR and prior-authorization requirements for high-performing physicians.
- Reduce unnecessary expenditures for inpatient hospital care by eliminating the duplicate payment for spinal hardware and the inflationary impact of coding improvement.
- Reduce unnecessary expenditures for ambulatory surgery by reducing the OMFS multiplier for procedures performed in freestanding ASCs.
- Reduce the incentives for inappropriate prescribing practices by curtailing in-office physician dispensing.
- Implement the pharmacy benefit network provisions.

Increase Accountability for Performance

Accountability for performance could be increased by making the following revisions in the Labor Code:

- Revise the MPN certification process to place accountability for meeting MPN standards on the entity contracting with the physician network.
- Strengthen DWC authorities to do the following:
  - Provide intermediate sanctions for failure to comply with MPN requirements.
  - Provide penalties for a claim administrator failing to comply with the data-reporting requirements.
- Modify the Labor Code to remove payers and MPNs from the definition of *individually identifiable data* so that performance on key measures can be publicly available.

Facilitate Monitoring and Oversight

Program oversight activities could be facilitated by the following:

- Provide DWC with more flexibility to add needed data elements to medical data reporting (e.g., revise the WCIS reporting requirements to require a unique identifier for each MPN).
- Require that medical cost-containment expenses be reported by category of cost (e.g., bill review, network leasing, UR, case management).
- Compile information on the types of medical services that are subject to UR denials and expedited hearings.
- Expand ongoing monitoring of system performance.

Increase Administrative Efficiency

Efficiency in the administration of medical benefits could be increased by the following:

- Use an external medical review organization to review medical-necessity determinations. A separate dispute-resolution process for medical-necessity determinations also creates a mechanism to monitor the quality of payer decisions and to identify areas in which expansions or revisions in the MTUS are needed.
- Explore best practices of other WC programs and health programs in carrying out medical cost-containment activities. For this study, we investigated best practices in medical-necessity dispute-resolution processes. Other cost-containment topics that might benefit from a review of best practices include the tools used by pharmacy benefit management programs, care coordination and catastrophic case management, profiling and other techniques that payers use to monitor E/M services and other utilization patterns and improve performance, and techniques for making UR most cost-effective and less administratively burdensome for high-performing physicians.

Issues Needing Additional Research

There are several aspects of the medical-treatment system that warrant additional investigation.

Cost of Care

An increased understanding is needed of the reasons behind the changes in the costs of medical care. This could be achieved by decomposing the WC cost experience into various components: price, utilization, claim volume and mix (industry and type of injury), and benchmarking the results to relevant WC and other health program experience. In the short run, this type of comparison will help explain the factors contributing to the changes in annual paid losses. In the long run, the methods developed to do so could be incorporated into a performance-monitoring system.

Quality of Care

With regard to quality of care, there are many significant challenges to developing appropriate measures for a performance-monitoring system. To date, very few measures assessing the appropriateness of care can be supported using only medical data. These, combined with utilization measures selected with input from providers and other stakeholders for common types of WC illnesses and injuries, could form the initial efforts to measure performance. These efforts could be enhanced and built on as new measures become available and the use of electronic medical records becomes common. As more information is reported through other measurement activities, such as the CMS Physician Quality Reporting System, the feasibility and stakeholder receptiveness to the inclusion of data reported to national performance-assessment efforts supported by all-payer data in a WC monitoring system should be assessed.

Work-Related Outcomes of Care

The literature concerning the impact of the reform provisions has focused on changes in the use and costs of medical services. Additional work is needed to understand how work-related outcomes, such as days lost from work and return to work, are affected by differences in patterns of service. This type of analysis will require linking transaction-level medical data with other administrative data sets.

Comparative Performance

Using what we learned during our stakeholder interviews, we identified selective contracting as an MPN best practice. Further research is needed to compare the pattern and costs of care under different contracting arrangements and to assess whether the narrow WC networks have better outcomes and cost-efficiency than broad networks.

References

ACOEM—*See* American College of Occupational and Environmental Medicine.

Adams, John L., Ateev Mehrotra, J. William Thomas, and Elizabeth A. McGlynn, "Physician Cost Profiling: Reliability and Risk of Misclassification," *New England Journal of Medicine*, Vol. 362, No. 11, 2010, pp. 1014–1021.

Airaksinen, O., J. I. Brox, C. Cedraschi, J. Hildebrandt, J. Klaber-Moffett, F. Kovacs, A. F. Mannion, S. Reis, J. B. Staal, H. Ursin, and G. Zanoli, "European Guidelines for the Management of Chronic Nonspecific Low Back Pain," *European Spine Journal*, Vol. 15, Suppl. 2, March 2006, pp. S192–S300.

American Academy of Actuaries, *Critical Issues in Health Reform: Minimum Loss Ratios*, Washington, D.C., February 2010. As of May 23, 2011:
http://www.actuary.org/pdf/health/loss_feb10.pdf

American College of Occupational and Environmental Medicine, *Occupational Medicine Practice Guidelines*, 2nd ed., Beverly Farms, Mass.: OEM Press, 2004.

———, *Occupational Medicine Practice Guidelines: Evaluation and Management of Common Health Problems and Functional Recovery of Workers*, Beverly Farms, Mass., 2011.

American Medical Association, *What Private Payers Do to Your Claim: Repricing and Claims Editing*, Sacramento, Calif.: National Healthcare Exchange Services, 2005. As of June 19, 2011:
http://www.nhxs.com/docs/files/File/nhxs_payor_report_for_AMA.pdf

Armon, Carmel, Charles E. Argoff, Jeffrey Samuels, and Misha-Miroslav Backonja, "Assessment: Use of Epidural Steroid Injections to Treat Radicular Lumbosacral Pain—Report of the Therapeutics and Technology Assessment Subcommittee of the American Academy of Neurology," *Neurology*, Vol. 68, No. 10, March 6, 2007, pp. 723–729.

Atlas, Steven J., and Richard A. Deyo, "Evaluating and Managing Acute Low Back Pain in the Primary Care Setting," *Journal of General Internal Medicine*, Vol. 16, No. 2, February 2001, pp. 120–131.

Baker, Christine, executive officer, Commission on Health and Safety and Workers' Compensation, "System Monitoring," memorandum to commissioners, Oakland, Calif., January 2011. As of April 29, 2011:
http://www.dir.ca.gov/chswc/Reports/2011/CHSWC_MemoOnSystemMonitoring.pdf

Bell, Rowen, American Academy of Actuaries, "Exposure Draft: Supplemental Health Care Exhibit," letter to Lou Felice, chair, Health Care Reform Solvency Impact Subgroup, National Association of Insurance Commissioners, May 17, 2010.

Billings, J., N. Parikh, and T. Mijanovich, "Instructions for Use of the ED Classification Algorithm," New York: Robert F. Wagner School of Public Service, undated. As of June 30, 2011:
http://archive.ahrq.gov/data/safetynet/nyualgorithm.doc

Boden, S. D., D. O. Davis, T. S. Dina, N. J. Patronas, and S. W. Wiesel, "Abnormal Magnetic-Resonance Scans of the Lumbar Spine in Asymptomatic Subjects: A Prospective Investigation," *Journal of Bone and Joint Surgery: American Volume*, Vol. 72, No. 3, March 1990, pp. 403–408.

Bureau of Labor Statistics, "Consumer Price Index-US City Average," undated.

California Code of Regulations, Title 16, Division 17, Section 1735.2.

California Department of Industrial Relations, "Division of Workers' Compensation," undated (a). As of May 26, 2011:
http://www.dir.ca.gov/DWC

———, "DWC Forums: Physician Fee Schedule Stakeholder Meeting Background Documents," undated (b). As of June 22, 2011: http://www.dir.ca.gov/dwc/DWCWCABForum/dwc_PhysicianFeeSchedule.htm

———, "Nonfatal Occupation Injuries and Illnesses in California," undated (c). As of May 24, 2011: http://www.dir.ca.gov/dlsr/nonfatal.htm

———, *Workers' Compensation Information System (WCIS): California EDI Implementation Guide for Medical Bill Payment Records*, version 1.0, Oakland, Calif., December 2005.

———, 18th Annual Division of Workers' Compensation Educational Conference, Los Angeles, Calif., February 24–25, 2011.

California Department of Insurance, "2010 CA Property and Casualty Market Share," undated. As of June 21, 2011:
http://www.insurance.ca.gov/0400-news/0200-studies-reports/0100-market-share/2010/index.cfm

California HealthCare Foundation, *California Employer Health Benefits Survey*, 2005. As of July 13, 2011: http://laborcenter.berkeley.edu/healthcare/resources/EmployerBenefitSurvey05.pdf

———, "Overuse of Emergency Departments Among Insured Californians," October 2006a. As of March 31, 2009:
http://www.chcf.org/publications/2006/10/overuse-of-emergency-departments-among-insured-californians

———, *California Employer Health Benefits Survey*, November 2006b. As of July 13, 2011: http://www.chcf.org/~/media/Files/PDF/E/PDF%20EmployerBenefitsSurvey06.pdf

———, *California Employer Health Benefits Survey*, December 2007. As of July 13, 2011: http://www.chcf.org/~/media/Files/PDF/E/PDF%20EmployerBenefitSurvey07.pdf

———, *California Employer Health Benefits Survey*, December 2008. As of July 13, 2011: http://www.chcf.org/~/media/Files/PDF/E/PDF%20EmployerBenefitsSurvey08.pdf

———, *California Employer Health Benefits Survey*, December 2009. As of July 13, 2011: http://www.chcf.org/~/media/Files/PDF/E/PDF%20EmployerBenefitsSurvey09.pdf

———, *California Employer Health Benefits Survey*, December 2010. As of June 30, 2011: http://www.chcf.org/publications/2010/12/california-employer-health-benefits-survey

California Senate Bill 228, Workers' Compensation, September 30, 2003. As of August 7, 2007: http://www.leginfo.ca.gov/pub/03-04/bill/sen/sb_0201-0250/sb_228_bill_20031001_chaptered.pdf

California Senate Bill 899, Workers' Compensation, April 19, 2004. As of August 8, 2007: http://info.sen.ca.gov/pub/03-04/bill/sen/sb_0851-0900/sb_899_bill_20040419_chaptered.pdf

Capen v. Shewry, 65 Cal. Rptr. 3d 890, 155 Cal. App. 4th 378, September 19, 2007.

Centers for Medicare and Medicaid Services, "Medicare Program; Revised Payment System Policies for Services Furnished in Ambulatory Surgical Centers (ASCs) Beginning in CY 2008," *Federal Register*, Vol. 72, No. 148, August 2, 2007, pp. 42470–42626. As of June 30, 2011:
http://www.federalregister.gov/articles/2007/08/02/07-3490/
medicare-program-revised-payment-system-policies-for-services-furnished-in-ambulatory-surgical

———, "Medicare Program; Hospital Inpatient Prospective Payment Systems for Acute Care Hospitals and the Long-Term Care Hospital Prospective Payment System Changes and FY2011 Rates; Provider Agreements and Supplier Approvals; and Hospital Conditions of Participation for Rehabilitation and Respiratory Care Services; Medicaid Program: Accreditation for Providers of Inpatient Psychiatric Services," *Federal Register*, Vol. 75, No. 157, August 16, 2010a, pp. 50042–50677. As of June 30, 2011:
http://www.federalregister.gov/articles/2010/08/16/2010-19092/
medicare-program-hospital-inpatient-prospective-payment-systems-for-acute-care-hospitals-and-the

———, *Evaluation and Management Services Guide*, ICN 006764, December 2010b. As of July 13, 2011: http://www.cms.gov/MLNProducts/downloads/eval_mgmt_serv_guide-ICN006764.pdf

Centers for Medicare and Medicaid Services and National Center for Health Statistics, *ICD-9-CM Official Guidelines for Coding and Reporting*, effective April 1, 2005.

CHCF—*See* California HealthCare Foundation.

Chou, Roger, Rongwei Fu, John A. Carrino, and Richard A. Deyo, "Imaging Strategies for Low-Back Pain: Systematic Review and Meta-Analysis," *Lancet*, Vol. 373, No. 9662, February 2009, pp. 463–472.

Chou, Roger, Amir Qaseem, Vincenza Snow, Donald Casey, J. Thomas Cross, Jr., Paul Shekelle, and Douglas K. Owens, "Diagnosis and Treatment of Low Back Pain: A Joint Clinical Practice Guideline from the American College of Physicians and the American Pain Society," *Annals of Internal Medicine*, Vol. 147, N. 7, October 2007, pp. 478–491.

CHSWC—*See* Commission on Health and Safety and Workers' Compensation.

CMS—*See* Centers for Medicare and Medicaid Services.

Commission on Health and Safety and Workers' Compensation, *Evaluating the QME Process: Is It Equitable and Efficient?* September 2010a. As of July 13, 2011:
http://www.dir.ca.gov/chswc/reports/2010/qmestudy.pdf

———, *CHSWC 2010 Annual Report*, Oakland, Calif., December 2010b. As of June 30, 2011:
http://www.dir.ca.gov/chswc/Reports/2010/CHSWC_AnnualReport2010.pdf

Coomer, Nicole M., Stacey Landes, Evelina Radeva, Carol A. Telles, Rui Yang, and Ramona P. Tanabe, *CompScope Medical Benchmarks for North Carolina*, 10th Edition, Cambridge, Mass.: Workers Compensation Research Institute, WC-10-27, July 2010.

Coventry Workers' Comp Services, undated home page. As of July 13, 2011:
http://www.coventrywcs.com/

Dallek, Geraldine, and Karen Pollitz, *External Review of Health Plan Decisions: An Update*, Washington, D.C.: Institute for Health Care Research and Policy, Georgetown University, 2000.

Dalton, Kathleen, Sara Freeman, and Arnold Bragg, *Refining Cost to Charge Ratios for Calculating APC and MS-DRG Relative Payment Weights*, Research Triangle Park, N.C.: RTI International, July 2008. As of October 31, 2008:
http://www.rti.org/reports/cms/HHSM-500-2005-0029I/PDF/
Refining_Cost_to_Charge_Ratios_200807_Final.pdf

Deshpande, A., A. D. Furlan, A. Mailis-Gagnon, S. Atlas, and D. Turk, "Opioids for Chronic Low-Back Pain," *Cochrane Database of Systematic Reviews 2007*, Vol. 3, No. CD004959, May 2007.

Deyo, Richard A., "Back Surgery: Who Needs It?" *New England Journal of Medicine*, Vol. 356, No. 22, May 31, 2007, pp. 2239–2243.

Deyo, Richard A., Sohail K. Mirza, and Brook I. Martin, "Back Pain Prevalence and Visit Rates: Estimates from U.S. National Surveys, 2002," *Spine*, Vol. 31, No. 23, November 1, 2006, pp. 2724–2727.

Deyo, Richard A., Sohail K. Mirza, Judith A. Turner, and Brook I. Martin, "Overtreating Chronic Back Pain: Time to Back Off?" *Journal of the American Board of Family Medicine*, Vol. 22, No. 1, 2009, pp. 62–68.

Dobson, Al, Joan DaVanzo, Maria Consunji, and Jawaria Gilani, *A Study of the Relative Work Content of Evaluation and Management Codes*, Falls Church, Va.: Lewin Group, April 29, 2003. As of June 30, 2011:
http://www.dir.ca.gov/dwc/medicalunit/StudyRelWorkContEvalMmgtCodes(draft).pdf

Fowles, J. B., E. J. Fowler, and C. Craft, "Validation of Claims Diagnoses and Self-Reported Conditions Compared with Medical Records for Selected Chronic Diseases," *Journal of Ambulatory Care Management*, Vol. 21, No. 1, January 1998, pp. 24–34.

Fowles, J. B., A. G. Lawthers, J. P. Weiner, D. W. Garnick, D. S. Petrie, and R. H. Palmer, "Agreement Between Physicians' Office Records and Medicare Part B Claims Data," *Health Care Financing Review*, Vol. 16, No. 4, Summer 1995, pp. 189–199.

Fox, Sharon E., Richard A. Victor, and Te-Chun Liu, *Comparing Outcomes for Injured Workers in Seven Large States*, Cambridge, Mass.: Workers Compensation Research Institute, WC-06-01, January 2006.

Gandhi, Tejal K., E. Francis Cook, Ann Louise Puopolo, Helen R. Burstin, Jennifer S. Haas, and Troyen A. Brennan, "Inconsistent Report Cards: Assessing the Comparability of Various Measures of the Quality of Ambulatory Care," *Medical Care*, Vol. 40, No. 2, February 2002, pp. 155–165.

Gatchel, Robert J., Peter B. Polatin, Carl Noe, Margaret Gardea, Carla Pulliam, and Judy Thompson, "Treatment- and Cost-Effectiveness of Early Intervention for Acute Low-Back Pain Patients: A One-Year Prospective Study," *Journal of Occupational Rehabilitation*, Vol. 13, No. 1, 2003, pp. 1–9.

Horner, Ronnie D., Janice A. Paris, John R. Purvis, and Frank H. Lawler, "Accuracy of Patient Encounter and Billing Information in Ambulatory Care," *Journal of Family Practice*, Vol. 33, No. 6, December 1991, pp. 593–598.

IAIABC—*See* International Association of Industrial Accident Boards and Commissions.

Institute of Medicine, Committee on Quality of Health Care in America, *Crossing the Quality Chasm: A New Health System for the 21st Century*, Washington, D.C.: National Academy Press, 2001. As of June 30, 2011: http://www.nap.edu/catalog/10027.html

International Association of Industrial Accident Boards and Commissions, *IAIABC EDI Implementation Guide for Medical Bill Payment Records*, Release 1, Madison, Wis., July 4, 2002.

IOM—*See* Institute of Medicine.

Ireland, John, and Alex Swedlow, *Research Update: Medical Provider Network Utilization in California Workers' Compensation*, Oakland, Calif.: California Workers' Compensation Institute, May 10, 2010.

Jarvick, Jeffrey G., William Hollingworth, Brook Martin, Scott S. Emerson, Darryl T. Gray, Steven Overman, David Robinson, Thomas Staiger, Frank Wessbecher, Sean D. Sullivan, William Kreuter, and Richard A. Deyo, "Rapid Magnetic Resonance Imaging vs Radiographs for Patients with Low Back Pain," *Journal of the American Medical Association*, Vol. 289, No. 21, 2003, pp. 2810–2818.

Kaiser Family Foundation, "California Employer Health Benefits Survey," undated. No longer available online.

KFF—*See* Kaiser Family Foundation.

Kominski, Gerald F., Nadereh Pourat, Dylan H. Roby, and Meghan E. Cameron, *Access to Medical Treatment in the California Workers' Compensation System*, 2006, Los Angeles, Calif.: UCLA Center for Health Policy Research, February 2007. As of June 30, 2011: http://www.healthpolicy.ucla.edu/pubs/Publication.aspx?pubID=216

Lewin Group, *Adapting the RBRVS Methodology to the California Workers' Compensation Physician Fee Schedule: Supplemental Report*, California Division of Workers' Compensation, March 3, 2010. As of July 1, 2011: http://www.dir.ca.gov/dwc/RBRVSLewinReport2010/RBRVSLewinReport2010.pdf

MacLean, Catherine H., Rachel Louie, Paul G. Shekelle, C. P. Roth, D. Saliba, T. Higashi, J. Adams, J. T. Chang, C. J. Kamberg, D. H. Solomon, R. T. Young, and N. S. Wenger, "Comparison of Administrative Data and Medical Records to Measure the Quality of Medical Care Provided to Vulnerable Older Patients," *Medical Care*, Vol. 44, No. 2, February 2006, pp. 141–148.

Martin, Brook I., Richard A. Deyo, Sohail K. Mirza, Judith A. Turner, Bryan A. Comstock, William Hollingworth, and Sean D. Sullivan, "Expenditures and Health Status Among Adults with Back and Neck Problems," *Journal of American Medical Association*, Vol. 299, No. 6, February 13, 2008, pp. 656–664.

Medicare Payment Advisory Commission, *Medicare Payment Policy: Report to the Congress*, March 2007. As of July 13, 2011: http://www.medpac.gov/documents/mar07_entirereport.pdf

———, *Medicare Payment Policy: Report to the Congress*, March 2010. As of July 18, 2011: http://www.medpac.gov/documents/Mar10_EntireReport.pdf

———, *Medicare Payment Policy: Report to the Congress*, March 2011a. As of July 13, 2011: http://www.medpac.gov/documents/mar11_entirereport.pdf

———, *A Data Book: Healthcare Spending and the Medicare Program*, Washington, D.C., June 2011b.

MedPAC—*See* Medicare Payment Advisory Commission.

Mike, Robert G., president, Workers' Compensation Insurance Rating Bureau of California, "California Workers' Compensation Insurance Pure Premium Rates, Regulations and Claims Cost Benchmark Amended Filing Effective January 1, 2010," letter to the Honorable Steve Poizner, San Francisco, Calif., September 22, 2009.

Miller, Paul, Denise Kendrick, Elaine Bentley, and Katherine Fielding, "Cost-Effectiveness of Lumbar Spine Radiography in Primary Care Patients with Low Back Pain," *Spine*, Vol. 27, No. 20, October 15, 2002, pp. 2291–2297.

Modic, Michael T., Nancy A. Obuchowski, Jeffrey S. Ross, Michael N. Brant-Zawadzki, Paul N. Groff, Daniel J. Mazanec, and Edward C. Benzel, "Acute Low Back Pain and Radiculopathy: MR Imaging Findings and Their Prognostic Role and Effect on Outcome," *Radiology*, Vol. 237, No. 2, 2005, pp. 597–604.

Mounce, K., "Back Pain," *Rheumatology*, Vol. 41, No. 1, 2002, pp. 1–5.

National Association of Insurance Commissioners, *Regulation for Uniform Definitions and Standardized Methodologies for Calculation of the Medical Loss Ratio for Plan Years 2011, 2012 and 2013 Per Section 2718(B) of the Public Health Service Act*, Washington, D.C., October 27, 2010. As of June 30, 2011:
http://www.naic.org/documents/committees_ex_mlr_reg_asadopted.pdf

National Association of Insurance Commissioners and Center for Insurance Policy and Research, *NAIC Response to Request for Information Regarding Section 2718 of the Public Health Service Act*, Washington, D.C., May 12, 2010. As of May 23, 2011:
http://www.insurance.naic.org/documents/committees_e_hrsi_hhs_response_mlr_adopted.pdf

Office of Statewide Health Planning and Development, "Emergency Department and Ambulatory Surgery Data," last revised December 20, 2010. As of May 24, 2011:
http://www.oshpd.ca.gov/HID/Products/EmerDeptData/index.html

Orthopedic Network News, Vol. 20, No. 4, October 2009.

Pennsylvania Department of Labor and Industry, *2004 Workers' Compensation Medical Access Study: Executive Summary*, Pittsburgh, Pa., 2005.

Pham, Hoangmai H., Bruce E. Landon, James D. Reschovsky, Beny Wu, and Deborah Schrag, "Rapidity and Modality of Imaging for Acute Low Back Pain in Elderly Patients," *Archives of Internal Medicine*, Vol. 169, No. 10, 2009, pp. 972–981.

Quan, Hude, Gerry A. Parsons, and William A. Ghali, "Assessing Accuracy of Diagnosis-Type Indicators for Flagging Complications in Administrative Data," *Journal of Clinical Epidemiology*, Vol. 57, No. 4, April 2004, pp. 366–372.

Rittenhouse, Diane R., Elizabeth Mertz, Dennis Keane, and Kevin Grumbach, "No Exit: An Evaluation of Measures of Physician Attrition," *Health Services Research*, Vol. 39, No. 5, October 2004, pp. 1571–1588.

Ritzwoller, Debra P., Laurie Crounse, Susan Shetterly, and Dale Rublee, "The Association of Comorbidities, Utilization and Costs for Patients Identified with Low Back Pain," *BMC Musculoskeletal Disorders*, Vol. 7, September 2006, p. 72.

Romano, Patrick S., "Can Administrative Data Be Used to Compare the Quality of Health Care?" *Medical Care Review*, Vol. 50, No. 4, Winter 1993, pp. 451–477.

Romano, Patrick S., and David H. Mark, "Bias in the Coding of Hospital Discharge Data and Its Implications for Quality Assessment," *Medical Care*, Vol. 32, No. 1, January 1994, pp. 81–90.

Sengupta, Ishita, Virginia Reno, and John F. Burton Jr., *Workers' Compensation: Benefits, Coverage, and Costs, 2006*, Washington, D.C.: National Academy of Social Insurance, August 2008. As of July 13, 2011:
http://www.nasi.org/research/2008/report-workers-compensation-benefits-coverage-costs-2006

———, *Workers' Compensation: Benefits, Coverage, and Costs, 2008*, Washington, D.C.: National Academy of Social Insurance, September 2010. As of July 13, 2011:
http://www.nasi.org/research/2010/report-workers-compensation-benefits-coverage-costs-2008

Sequist, Thomas D., Eric C. Schneider, Angela Li, William H. Rogers, and Dana Gelb Safran, "Reliability of Medical Group and Physician Performance Measurement in the Primary Care Setting," *Medical Care*, Vol. 49, No. 2, February 2011, pp. 126–131.

Smith-Bindman, Rebecca, Diana L. Miglioretti, and Eric B. Larson, "Rising Use of Diagnostic Medical Imaging in a Large Integrated Health System," *Health Affairs*, Vol. 27, No. 6, 2008, pp. 1491–1502.

Solberg, Leif I., Karen I. Engebretson, Joann M. Sperl-Hillen, Mary C. Hroscikoski, and Patrick J. O'Connor, "Are Claims Data Accurate Enough to Identify Patients for Performance Measures or Quality Improvement? The Case of Diabetes, Heart Disease, and Depression," *American Journal of Medical Quality*, Vol. 21, No. 4, July–August 2006, pp. 238–245.

Sullivan, Mark D., Mark J. Edlund, Diane Steffick, and Jürgen Unützer, "Regular Use of Prescribed Opioids: Association with Common Psychiatric Disorders," *Pain*, Vol. 119, No. 1–3, pp. 95–103.

Swedlow, Alex, and John Ireland, *California Workers' Compensation Reform Outcomes, Research Update*, Part 1: *Changes in Medical Cost Containment Payments Accident Years 2002–2007*, Oakland, Calif.: California Workers' Compensation Institute, October 2008.

Swedlow, Alex, John Ireland, and L. B. Gardner, *Analysis of California Workers' Compensation Reforms*, Part 4: *Changes in Medical Payments, Accident Years 2002 to 2007 Claims Experience*, Oakland, Calif.: California Workers' Compensation Institute, June 2009.

Swedlow, Alex, John Ireland, and Gregory Johnson, *Prescribing Patterns of Schedule II Opioids in California Workers' Compensation*, Oakland, Calif.: California Workers' Compensation Institute, March 2011.

Victor, Richard A., *Evidence of Effectiveness of Policy Levers to Contain Medical Costs in Workers' Compensation*, Cambridge, Mass.: Workers Compensation Research Institute, 2003.

Victor, Richard A., Peter S. Barth, and Te-Chun Liu, *Outcomes for Injured Workers in California, Massachusetts, Pennsylvania, and Texas*, Cambridge, Mass.: Workers Compensation Research Institute, WC-03-07, December 2003.

WCIRB—*See* Workers' Compensation Insurance Rating Bureau of California.

WCRI—*See* Workers Compensation Research Institute.

Wickizer, Thomas M., Gary M. Franklin, Robert D. Mootz, Deborah Fulton-Kehoe, Roy Plaeger-Brockway, Diana Drylie, Judith A. Turner, and Terri Smith-Weller, "A Communitywide Intervention to Improve Outcomes and Reduce Disability Among Injured Workers in Washington State," *Milbank Quarterly*, Vol. 82, No. 3, September 2004, pp. 547–567.

Wickizer, Thomas M., Jeanne M. Sears, Dolly A. John, Beryl A. Schulman, and Janessa M. Graves, *Access, Quality, and Outcomes of Health Care in the California Workers' Compensation System, 2008*, Seattle, Wash.: University of Washington School of Public Health, 2009. As of July 1, 2011:
http://www.dir.ca.gov/dwc/MedicalTreatmentCA2008/2008_CA_WC_Access_Study_UW_report.pdf

Workers' Compensation Insurance Rating Bureau of California, *2003 California Workers' Compensation Insured Losses and Expenses*, San Francisco, Calif.: Workers' Compensation Insurance Rating Bureau of California, June 2004. As of July 1, 2011:
https://wcirbonline.org/wcirb/wcirb_wire/pdf/2004/11759_1_report_CY2003.pdf

———, *WCIRB Summary of Policy Year Statistics: 2010 Release*, June 14, 2010a. As of July 1, 2011:
https://wcirbonline.org/wcirb/resources/data_reports/pdf/Bulletin_201006_Policy_Year_Statistics.pdf

———, *2009 California Workers' Compensation Losses and Expenses*, San Francisco, Calif.: Workers' Compensation Insurance Rating Bureau of California, June 22, 2010b. As of July 1, 2011:
https://wcirbonline.org/wcirb/resources/data_reports/pdf/2009_loss_and_expenses.pdf

———, *California Workers' Compensation Uniform Statistical Reporting Plan—1995: Title 10, California Code of Regulations, Section 2318.6*, January 1, 2011. As of May 23, 2011:
https://wcirbonline.org/wcirb/root/pdf/usrp_ic_regs_only.pdf

Workers Compensation Research Institute, *The Anatomy of Workers' Compensation Medical Costs and Utilization in California*, Cambridge, Mass., 5th ed., November 2005.

———, *Anatomy of WC Medical Costs and Utilization in Florida*, Cambridge, Mass., 6th ed., February 2007.

————, The Anatomy of Workers' Compensation Medical Costs and Utilization in California, Cambridge, Mass., 7th ed., January 2009.

Wynn, Barbara O., Adopting Medicare Fee Schedules: Considerations for the California Workers' Compensation Program, Santa Monica, Calif.: RAND Corporation, MR-1776-ICJ, 2004. As of July 1, 2011: http://www.rand.org/pubs/monograph_reports/MR1776.html

————, Inpatient Hospital Services: An Update on Services Provided Under California's Workers' Compensation Program, Santa Monica, Calif.: RAND Corporation, WR-629-CHSWC, 2009. As of July 1, 2011: http://www.rand.org/pubs/working_papers/WR629.html

Wynn, Barbara O., and Giacomo Bergamo, Payment for Hardware Used in Complex Spinal Procedures Under California's Official Medical Fee Schedule for Injured Workers, Santa Monica, Calif.: RAND Corporation, WR-301-ICJ, 2005. As of July 1, 2011: http://www.rand.org/pubs/working_papers/WR301.html

Wynn, Barbara O., Giacomo Bergamo, Rebecca Shaw, Soeren Mattke, and Allard E. Dembe, Medical Care Provided California's Injured Workers: An Overview of the Issues, Santa Monica, Calif.: RAND Corporation, WR-394-ICJ, 2007. As of July 1, 2011: http://www.rand.org/pubs/working_papers/WR394.html

Wynn, Barbara O., Peter S. Hussey, and Teague Ruder, Policy Options for Addressing Medicare Payment Differentials Across Ambulatory Settings, Santa Monica, Calif.: RAND Corporation, TR-979-ASPE, forthcoming.

Wynn, Barbara O., and Melony E. Sorbero, Pay for Performance in California's Workers' Compensation Medical Treatment System: An Assessment of Options, Challenges, and Potential Benefits, Santa Monica, Calif.: RAND Corporation, OP-229-CHSWC, 2008. As of July 1, 2011: http://www.rand.org/pubs/occasional_papers/OP229.html

Yang, Rui, Nicole M. Coomer, Stacey Landes, Evelina Radeva, Carol A. Telles, and Ramona P. Tanabe, Monitoring the Impact of Regulatory Changes in California: CompScope Medical Benchmarks, 10th Edition, Cambridge, Mass.: Workers Compensation Research Institute, WC-10-19, July 2010.

Yang, Rui, Nicole M. Coomer, Evelina Radeva, Bogdan Savych, Carol A. Telles, and Ramona P. Tanabe, CompScope Benchmarks for California, 11th Edition, Cambridge, Mass.: Workers Compensation Research Institute, WC-11-02, January 2011.